HOLLYWOOD
AND ME

*To Brian
& Katie*

LA/06

» *Bernie Rothman*

HOLLYWOOD
AND ME

*Just keep
on laughing —
++ T
Bernie*

MY WILD RIDE

THROUGH THE

GOLDEN AGE

OF TELEVISION

GREYSTONE BOOKS
Douglas & McIntyre Publishing Group
Vancouver/Toronto/Berkeley

Greystone Books
A division of Douglas & McIntyre Ltd.
2323 Quebec Street, Suite 201
Vancouver, British Columbia
Canada V5T 4S7
www.greystonebooks.com

Library and Archives Canada Cataloguing in Publication
Rothman, Bernard, 1933–
Hollywood and me : my wild ride through the golden age of television / Bernie
Rothman.

Includes index.
ISBN-13: 978-1-55365-202-1 · ISBN-10: 1-55365-202-9

1. Rothman, Bernard, 1933-. 2. Entertainers—United States—Anecdotes. 3.
Television producers and directors—United States—Biography. 4. Television writers—United States—Biography.
5. Television writers—Canada—Biography. I. Title.
PN1992.4.R68A3 2006   791.4502′33′092   C2006-902980-6

Editing by Nancy Flight
Cover and text design by Naomi MacDougall
Cover illustration © Trinette Reed/CORBIS
Printed and bound in Canada by Friesens
Printed on acid-free paper that is forest friendly
(100% post-consumer recycled paper)
and has been processed chlorine free.
Distributed in the U.S. by Publishers Group West

Photographs of Danny Kaye, Rudolf Nureyev, and
Gene Kelly: MichaelOchsArchives.com
Photograph of Carl Reiner and Bernie Rothman: Amy Tierny/Alex Berliner Studio
All other photographs: courtesy of Bernie Rothman

"Is That All There Is," words and music by Jerry Lieber and Mike Stoller © 1966
(renewed) JERRY LIEBER MUSIC and MIKE STOLLER MUSIC.
All rights reserved. Reproduced by permission.

Every effort has been made to trace accurate ownership of copyright text
and visual material used in this book. Errors or omissions will be corrected in
subsequent editions, provided notification is sent to the publisher.

We gratefully acknowledge the financial support of the Canada Council for
the Arts, the British Columbia Arts Council, and the Government
of Canada through the Book Publishing Industry Development Program
(BPIDP) for our publishing activities.

**this book is for bobbi
and for our amazing kids**

★ ★ ★

*the author wishes to thank
Nancy Flight
a brilliant editor who believed in me
even when I didn't
the intrepid Rob Sanders
who bought this book
before it was one
and David Suzuki
a good friend, a great man
a true citizen of our planet*

CONTENTS

PREFACE

∨

THIS IS NOT A MEMOIR. RETIRED GEN-
erals write memoirs. Prime ministers
write memoirs. Glamorous movie stars write memoirs. (They
don't actually write them; they pay someone else to.) Only
famous people write memoirs, because people want to read
them. Publishers aren't stupid, you know. So if a memoir is
what you're expecting, read no further. This isn't one.

What is it, then, if it's not a memoir? I don't know. I know
what it isn't. It isn't a symphony, it isn't an oil painting, and
it isn't a freight train. Maybe we'll call it an un-memoir,
okay?

Why am I writing this—this indescribable thing that I
can't even find a category for? (I know, I know—never end
a sentence with a preposition—big deal!) Why? Because
my wife told me to. I always do what my wife tells me. Not
at first, but eventually. This happened in the middle of
one of my endless stories about some celebrity I'd worked
with. I think it was Judy Garland. No, not Judy, Jack Benny.
Anyway, somebody dead. I'd told her the story umpteen

times, and her eyes were beginning to glaze over. I waited for her to interrupt me with her usual, "Bottom line—get to the bottom line!" But she didn't. Instead she said, "Why don't you write your memoirs?"

For a moment I was shocked into lucidity: "You gotta be kiddin'!"

"Your stories are interesting," she went on. "You've worked with fabulous people. You should write your memoirs."

"Never!" I asserted vociferously, nearly waking her up. "Memoirs are just an ego trip—I hate the idea!"

I was lying, of course. I loved the idea but figured if my stories were in print, no one would ever listen to me tell them again. "Besides," I added weakly, "they're so personal; who would publish them?"

"Someone smart," she said, and left it at that. She always "left it at that" when she knew she had me.

I couldn't get rid of the thought: the unlikely tale of a starstruck kid from Montreal, fighting his way up the Hollywood ladder, right to the top—well, not quite to the top—but better than halfway up—and working as a respected television producer with the most lustrous stars of his time. Told with appropriate humility, of course. This would be no self-serving memoir, no ego trip. More like history, don't you think?

Did I mention my wife has a PhD in psychology? She's very smart. Smarter about the public taste than I am. So I took her suggestion very seriously. For about ten minutes. Then I realized there was work involved. Real writing. I mean with words—the one kind of writing I hate! Plus, it would all be on spec. Okay, you try it—try writing 80,000 words with no guarantee of a sale.

So then a funny thing happens: Suzuki comes into town. No, it's not funny that he comes into town, it's funny what happens over dinner. Suzuki is Dr. David Suzuki, the world's greatest scientist/environmentalist/media star/salmon fisherman. And he's my friend. We've done a couple of TV specials together, gone fishing—I love the guy. And I admire him so much for the amazing work he does for our planet. So we're out having one of our delightful dinners, and I'm telling him one of my stories—I think it was about how Rudolf Nureyev almost singlehandedly destroyed my career on a CBS dance special—is this what they call name dropping? Anyway, I notice David isn't really listening, he's waiting to interrupt. "I know, I know," I say before he can. "I've got to stop telling these boring, self-serving stories."

David's jaw drops. "That's not what I was going to say," he counters.

"You would have, if you'd thought of it," I say, chuckling with uncharacteristic self-deprecation.

"I was going to tell you that you've got to write your memoirs," says David, two days after my wife made the same suggestion. I am stunned. Could this be another person who doesn't want to listen to my "humorous anecdotes" in person?

"Come on, David . . ." I plead.

But he persists: "No, I mean it—your stories are terrific. I'm gonna talk to my publisher when I go back. So get started!"

I remember what George Burns told me that first day of rehearsal for his special. He had just shocked the world with a virtuoso acting job—his first—at the age of seventy-nine, in *Sunshine Boys*. "George, you became a great actor overnight!" I say. "What's the secret?"

"Sincerity," he says, without a moment's hesitation, then puffs on his cigar. "Once you learn how to fake that, the rest is easy."

David Suzuki usually means what he says. He's an absolute icon in most countries of the semicivilized world, and he's written over forty books that got published. So when he says he'll talk to his publisher, get started, he means it.

Well, he did and I have. But it's not a memoir—remember that. I'll probably figure out what it is by the end of the book, so quit bugging me.

THE SHOW

MUST GO ON—

OR MUST IT?

*H*OW DO I LIKE LIVING IN HOLLY-wood, people ask. And I tell them I don't live there. Never did—hardly anyone does. It's a pretty rundown place, most of it—kind of seedy. I've lived in Beverly Hills, Malibu, Santa Monica, London, Sydney, Montreal—never in the big H. So why call my book *Hollywood and Me*? Because Hollywood's a great metaphor. It means glamor, film stars, movies, TV, the Oscars. Who would buy a book called *Fargo, North Dakota, and Me*? Doesn't have the same ring, does it? So think of L.A. as the center of the film and television world, where the deals are made, and you'll know why I moved here forty years ago. I wanted to make those deals.

Do I like living here? Great residential areas, plenty of restaurants and night life, year-round outdoor activities, pretty girls, and an average temperature of 72°F—what's to hate? Okay, there is the occasional downside. Minor ones. Like when an earthquake comes along and wipes out your house. Or a mudslide or a tidal wave or a forest fire. Big deal, you've got insurance, don't you? Oh, sorry.

But some things happen in Hollywood that couldn't happen anywhere else. For instance:

It's twilight as I come out of Moustache Café in Hollywood. I've just had a drink with Tricia Taw, Bob Stivers's amazing assistant. (Bob, a friend, created the People's Choice Awards. Now he and I are doing *Command Performance* for CBS.) As Trish and I turn off Melrose Avenue onto a quiet side street, an old-model Camaro screeches to a halt ahead of us. Three heavyset tough guys pour out of the car onto the sidewalk, blocking the path ahead. And if I'm not mistaken, *they're pointing their shotgun right at us!*

"Gimme all you got!" the lead thug shouts, right in our faces. Tricia's smart, doesn't look the guy in the eye. I go numb and just hand him everything in my pockets. They grab Tricia's handbag and everything I've got they think is valuable—there isn't much—four crumpled one-dollar bills and a Rolex they know is a knockoff. All the while they're screaming, and I can actually hear Tricia's knees knocking. It's over in a couple of minutes as the thugs take off in their beat-up Camaro. Shock! They've taken practically nothing. Except:

"Shit! They got my car keys, Trish! I'll have to call Bobbi to come get us."

At this precise moment, the getaway car comes to a screeching halt. The car door opens.

"Hey mister," one of the thugs says amiably, "—your keys." He tosses my key ring out in the middle of the sidewalk.

"Hey, thanks," I yell back as I pick up the keys. But they're gone.

BUT THE WILDEST thing about living in Hollywood isn't the earthquakes or the mudslides or the muggers. It's the parties.

My first Hollywood party is at the elegant Beverly Hills home of Stanley Prager, Danny Kaye's new producer. I'm new to the writing staff and thrilled to be invited. What a treat! We all dress up in our finest, dine al fresco on a five-course gourmet dinner catered by Chasen's (arguably Hollywood's most famous restaurant), then sit around the pool sipping our cognacs and swapping war stories. It isn't wild or raucous or anything like that. We aren't drunk or even high. Just a friendly group, enjoying ourselves on a balmy summer evening.

Then it happens. Paul Mazursky's lovely wife, Betsy, dressed in her beautiful Grecian gown, walks right into the swimming pool. No, she doesn't dive in; she isn't pushed. She just calmly walks down the stairs at the shallow end, keeps on walking till she practically disappears. Now why would this lovely, soft-spoken woman walk into a swimming pool, dressed head to toe in silk chiffon? True, she'd been complaining all evening about the humidity, and, oh well, this is Hollywood.

Another evening, my friend Gayle is taking me to a party at Brooke Palance's house. (Brooke is actor Jack Palance's daughter). Leonard Cohen, my closest pal, has just moved to Hollywood, and I ask Gayle if we can invite him along. "I'll check with Brooke," says Gayle, and she does. "Brooke says she'd be honored."

So I invite Leonard, who says he'll come by to pick us up in half an hour. But he calls right back, asks if there'll be room at the party for one more guest. When I tell Gayle who Cohen wants to bring, we agree we won't have to clear it with Brooke. We show up at the party with Leonard Cohen on one arm and Cohen's friend, Bob Dylan, on the other. And no one bats an eyelash.

Happens every day in this town. No one's normal here.

Not even the cops. One day I'm whipping along Fountain Avenue around fifty-five an hour, when I get pulled over by this very burly motorcycle cop. With a jaw as wide as his sidecar. So don't mess with this guy.

"Sorry Mister," he says, real polite. "Gotta cite ya. Goin' too fast not to."

"What was I doin', officer?" I ask.

"Don't know exactly," he tells me. "Close to sixty, I figure, 'cause it took me four blocks to catch you." He's writing the ticket.

"Wish you'd told me," I say. "I woulda slowed down so you could catch up."

He laughs. "Hey—you a comedy writer?"

"Used to be," I tell him. "I'm a producer now."

"Oh, a producer," he says, impressed. He hands me the ticket. "Sorry about this, but it's my job, sir." Begins to walk away, then turns back. "Kinda curious—what do you produce?"

"Right now I'm producing a new series—just on the air a couple of months—a '50s comedy, called *Sha Na Na*."

"*Sha Na Na*?" he says, horrified. "I should give you two tickets!"

Like I said, it happens every day in this town. Everyone's a bit loopy here. But it's where I've always wanted to be—in Hollywood, making up dreams for people.

BIRTH OF A

PLAYWRIGHT

*H*ER NAME IS SORREL. SHE'S TALL, slender, very pretty. And I'm mad for her. We make up plays and act out the parts—the cowboy and the Indian princess, the doctor and the nurse, the teacher and the student—every conceivable combination, each very different from the other. Except the endings: each play ends with a kiss.

It is the summer I turn seven. Sorrel is six. Our parents have back-to-back cottages on Old Orchard Beach in Maine. I learn how to swim and, thanks to Sorrel, how to kiss. I also learn I can make up plays, something I hang on to for years. Can't hang on to Sorrel, though. She marries one of the world's leading scientists and, as far as I know, lives a happy life without making up plays. As for me—I never know whether it was Sorrel I fell in love with or the plays. But if you're looking for a way to break into the entertainment business, start young and find yourself a girl to make up plays with. Maybe you'll marry her, maybe you won't. Maybe you'll wind up in showbiz, maybe you won't. But I guarantee you'll enjoy the kisses.

SUMMER ROMANCES DON'T usually last. That summer in Old Orchard Beach ends, and so does my torrid play-making romance with the lovely Sorrel. I once ride my bike over to her house, which is nearby, but it isn't the same. Apparently, we need the beach for our muse. So my budding career as a playwright/Casanova comes to an abrupt end.

That summer is the year we move. From a cozy house in middle-class Outremont to a baronial mansion in upper-class Westmount. My father had immigrated to Montreal from Poland a decade and a half earlier. All by himself. With a few paltry kopecks his family had saved for him to make the trip. He couldn't speak a single word of English. He was fourteen years old. Twelve years later he's a millionaire. How did he do it? Guts and brains.

He starts out sweeping floors for a small-time dress manu-facturer. But he's bright and works tirelessly, so he moves up. Pretty soon he's a shipper, filling orders for dress stores all over the country. A few years more and he is in the cutting room—he has the all-important job of cutting material into patterns that are then sewn into dresses. That job pays real money. Like eighteen dollars a week. (It's the Depression.) Maybe twenty if he will stay on with the firm. But he is far too ambitious *not* to go into business for himself. So after seven years of toiling for his boss, he's learned enough, and saved enough, to invest in a dress business of his own. Instant success. And he never looks back.

He marries a beautiful young Russian girl, every bit as smart as he is. (Of course, he doesn't find that out till *after* they're married.) She is nineteen and gorgeous. Couple of years later she gives birth to my brother, Mel; three years later, they have me (does Mel ever forgive them for that?). Then, finally, the blessing—my kid sister, Renee. Whew! They need a bigger house.

They find one that's beyond my father's wildest dreams. But not beyond my mother's. On two and a half rolling acres atop Westmount Mountain—the most magnificent house I've ever seen. Twelve thousand square feet, give or take a few inches, a hallway that domes at four stories high, all in harlequin Italian marble. Four bedrooms with seven bathrooms, five fireplaces, huge living room, dining room, a bar, a library, a bowling alley in the basement, a billiard room, a greenhouse, servants' quarters with three bedrooms and a den—gorgeous! It wins all kinds of architectural prizes. That's how we live. With a maid, a butler, and a Chinese cook. (Am I showing off?)

The year is 1940. There's a war on, but you can't tell by Westmount. The town has everything going at full steam— gorgeous estates, sumptuous parks, chauffeured limousines, elegant boutiques, private schools—everything. Except Jews.

For some people that doesn't present a problem. But I can't get home from school without a fight. Kids can be cruel. Especially privileged ones. But if you're fighting every day, you get good at it. And pretty soon they stop calling you "Christ-killer," for fear they might be next on your list.

My brother, Mel, has a steeper hill to climb. He had polio when he was a kid, fought back bravely. He's determined to lead a normal life, and he isn't easily intimidated. Secretly, he takes boxing lessons, and the first kid that calls him a dirty name learns a bitter lesson. Inflicting one broken nose is all it takes to level Mel's playing field. He never has to inflict a second. He's a man of courage.

After that, my brother, my sister, and I grow up peacefully, and believe it or not, ecumenically, in Westmount. My friends include guys with names like McCullogh and Ferrabee, as well as Cohen and Rosengarten. Likewise, the girls. I like them all, no matter what they do with their Sunday mornings.

All through our childhood, Mel looks after me like an extra parent. Which is just as well since my parents fight like a couple of children. Mel grows into a very fine lawyer and is appointed to the bench of the Superior Court at a very young age. Has to take a big cut in salary to do it, too, but he is passionate about law and dedicates his life to it.

Then there is my other sibling. Almost from the day my parents bring her home from the hospital, my kid sister, Renee, is my very dearest friend. She's cute and pink and cuddly, and I know she'll always be on my side. We'll just laugh and play and have fun. I'll take her for rides in my little red wagon, and I'll never bully her like my older brother and my mother and my father bully me. She'll just be my baby sister, and I'll love her the rest of my life.

Renee is six years younger than me. She grows up tall and pretty and has several successful careers—as an expert food writer, a guide at the United Nations, an editor with a Toronto publishing firm, a PR executive with the Toronto Symphony, an impresario for some of Canada's leading classical musicians. All this, while bringing up three kids, being a good wife to her handsome South African husband, and entertaining a host of loquacious Mah-Jongg cronies. She's just amazing. More amazing is the bond between us—the warmth, the loyalty—it just keeps on growing.

My sister is a person of unusually happy temperament. But when she is fifteen, she has her first heartbreak. Handsome, charming Gordon, after courting her avidly for six months, finally gets her. And drops her six months later. Renee is shattered. Each night she comes to the dinner table, positively morose. She sits sadly at my father's side, picking at her food, barely saying a word. Which is hard to do, because, whereas our dinners are formal, conversations are very spirited. Of course, the family knows why our littlest member is so depressed. That rascal Gordon has jilted her! But all attempts at cheering her up fail miserably. She doesn't want to talk, so we leave her to mourn alone.

It is one of those dinners when Renee is particularly morose that my father leans over, strokes her gently on the shoulder, and in a voice brimming with compassion, says: "Don't worry, dear—Daddy'll buy you a better one."

Much laughter. And that's the end of Renee's depression.

I do remember one irritating moment, and only one, when I actually get mad at my baby sister. It happens during her teens. Renee is blabbering on the telephone for a very long time. About nothing. I stand beside her, real close, waiting for my turn, giving her the wind-up signal, giving it faster and faster. Yes, I'm taunting her. Renee keeps watching me out of the corner of her eye, and then—blamm!—right over my head with the phone receiver. I scream. My mother comes running in. There is blood trickling down my fore-head (not a lot, but a little). Mom takes one look, delivers a smack across Renee's face, and my sister goes down for the count—well, no, not really. We both survive. And we learn the true meaning of love for a sibling. Besides, it *was* my fault, wasn't it?

MY MOTHER BRINGS culture into our family—we go to concerts, plays, opera, and ballet, and, most important, we three Rothlings take piano lessons. My brother and my sister are the lucky ones. It is determined early on that they have no talent, or precious little, anyway. So our piano teacher gives up on them after a year or two. I am deemed to be very musical, which gives me the privilege of slaving away at Mozart and Vivaldi for the next hundred and fifty years while my poor untalented siblings serve a life sentence of baseball, skiing, and other frothy entertainments. But Mom is right. My music gives a spine to my life, while my poor siblings have to concentrate on being normal. Who wants to be normal when you can be a fruitcake your whole life?

Piano. I love the instrument. Just hate practicing, that's all. My mother has to sit beside me night after night to make sure I practice. Love the attention, hate the work. Have a great teacher—Michel Hirvy, a passionate Pole, who turns out some great pianists. His love for music is inspiring. Still, I never practice. So my lessons are very frustrating for Mr. Hirvy. "I should throw you out," he yells at me, "but I need the money!"

He never stops being supportive of my talent. Which means my mother never lets me give up the damn lessons.

In the meantime, I discover playacting. In junior high, I win the comedy lead in a one-acter. At summer camp, I'm always one of the leads in the "big musical." Nothing to do with talent. Let's face it—I'm a monstrous showoff. Always was.

At Camp Wabikon, in my early teens, I come into my own. I meet the adorable Ruth. We're crazy about each other. She's very pretty and as talented as any girl from Toronto can be. Plays wonderful classical piano and always encourages my performing. But she doesn't know how to make up plays, so we never kiss. At that age, relationships don't last unless you kiss.

Happily, there's a dramatics counselor at Wabikon who thinks I'm talented. In fact, there are two. Sid Wallman let me help him with the Saturday night variety shows. Gawd, they were fun! Staging all those songs from Judy Garland movies—"Clang, clang, clang went the trolley"—no I don't sing it, I play the conductor who pulls the cord. (Who'd ever dream I'd wind up in Hollywood twenty years later, on Judy Garland's writing staff?) The shows are made up of pop songs and comedy sketches—maybe a dozen of us in the cast, performing pretty campy material, but it gives us a taste of the stage.

Then there are the plays, directed by an excellent professional actor, Lloyd Bochner. (You may remember him playing Joan Collins's husband in *Dynasty*. Fine actor.) Lloyd directs me in a potboiler mystery called *Shivering Shocks*. I play a Scotland Yard detective. Years later, I direct Lloyd in a potboiler mystery on television, and he plays the role of—you got it—a Scotland Yard detective. Turnabout *is* fair play, isn't it?

Looking back, I'm sure my mentors saw more chutzpah in me than talent. Which is all you need at that age. I have no fear of performing. The first song I perform solo on stage is "I'm Just a Girl Who Can't Say No"—from the musical *Oklahoma*. The audience loves it—laughs all the way through—maybe it's my dress. And I never get over the excitement of a cheering audience. That's it—I got the bug.

At Wabikon, Leonard Cohen and I become friends. We both adore girls, have our adolescent crushes, begin writing poems. Love poems. Mine are very syrupy:

Who is that young maiden I love from afar
She glows like a candle, shines like a star
But as she draws nearer, her warmth, I'm afraid
Turns cold as the evening in darkness and shade.

Maybe it impresses the adorable Ruth—though I doubt it—but I know my poems aren't very good. Cohen's poetry is much better. (You probably guessed that.) He is kind about mine, but the comparison is obvious. Or odious. Something. Anyway, I stop writing poetry and begin writing lyrics instead. It's the same kind of thing, just not as deep. I soon find I'm as good at lyrics as I'm bad at poetry. Especially funny lyrics. I write them speedily, easily, and well. And that, dear friends, earns me a songwriter's living for many a year.

SCHOOL'S OUT,
SCHOOL'S IN

*M*ONTREAL IN THE '40S IS NUTS. Night clubs, jazz clubs, underground gambling clubs, cafés and bistros, pool halls, beer halls, spareribs at Ruby Foos, spaghetti at FDR's, smoked meat at Ben's, Frank Sinatra at the Chez Paree, Lena Horne at the Esquire Show Bar, Oscar Peterson at Victoria Hall, Paul Bley, a guy who can play, the occasional gay—and Maury Kaye gets put away for smoking M.J. Dancing girls at the Bellevue, Rosita & Dino at the Normandy, Dixieland at Rockheads, burlesque at the Gayety, symphony halls, the Beaux Arts Ball, girls on call, culture all around you, and brothels, brothels everywhere—high class, low class, any class, but high school class is empty on Friday afternoons when Lili St. Cyr brings her sinuous naked body to the stage.

It's a staccato city, Canada's largest—maybe a million and a half—70 percent French, in Quebec Province, which is 90 percent French. So we anglophones are in the minority, and I'm in a minority in the minority. It's mostly Catholic, but Jewish kids are schooled by the Protestant School Board, which is so English it's like they never left Knightsbridge.

So there we are, an island of non-Protestants, in a sea of Catholics, in a province that really doesn't want to be in a country, which isn't a country. It's a dominion. What the hell is that—a dominion? Nobody knows. You can't blame the French. Canada has a national anthem that's all about saving the King of England, and we don't even have our own flag.

But I'll tell you this—Montreal is a helluva lot more fun to grow up in than the rest of Canada. You eat better, play harder, drink heartier, laugh louder, work less, play more. The women are chic-er, warmer, sexier, and more likely to say "yes."

So that's Montreal in 1949, the year I graduate from high school.

MCGILL UNIVERSITY IS in the heart of downtown Montreal, a bustling beehive of a campus, as charming as any of the Ivy League schools. Darn near two hundred years old, and for most of those years, it's been Canada's top university. Which makes it a top school worldwide. There were sixty-five hundred students when I went to McGill. Close to thirty thousand now.

My parents argue about whether or not I should go to college.

"He doesn't need it!" says my father. "He's coming into my business, and I can teach him everything he needs to know about business."

"He's going to college!" shouts my mom. "He's a very talented boy, and he's not going to learn culture in the dress business!" She has that right.

"Please, Nellie—he doesn't need culture. College will only give him grand ideas." And, of course, it does. But my mother wins out. Thank God!

It's always assumed I'll go in with Dad. He thinks I have good business sense and instinctively know how to sell. I don't agree with him on either point, but what the hell—he and my brother don't get along, and my sister, who has great business sense, is a *girl,* and business is not what my folks have in mind for her.

I work summers in Dad's dress business—kind of an exciting place—stylish, unpredictable, lots of action and I like it. At college, I'm not much interested in economics or accounting or marketing. So I minor in English lit and philosophy and come out with a pretty balanced education.

But it's McGill's rich extracurricular life that shapes my career, not the academics. And the community of creative people—William Shatner, Leonard Cohen, Jack Shayne, Brian MacDonald, Norma Springford, Bob Robinson, John Pratt, Jim Domville, Ron Clarke, Ian Ross, Roy Wolvin, Ken Rosenberg—they give me a taste for theater I can never get out of my system.

It begins at Activities Night, the eve of the first day of school. We hang out all night at the dumpy old Students' Union, wandering from booth to booth, introducing ourselves to the various extracurricular clubs. There's a club for everything: a debating society, music societies, a Spanish club, a French club, five different drama societies, a hang-gliding club, a Caribbean club, a landscaping society—you name it, they've got it. I'm recruited by the debating society (my brother, Mel, is president), and the Red and White Revue—Canada's best-known college show. Bill Shatner is producing this year.

I try debating first. It's expected of me, my brother being so good at it. But it's a wipeout. Three debates, three losses. It's my brother's field, not mine. I can't compete.

Then I try script writing. I join a bunch of guys Shatner enlisted to write his musical revue—*Red, Hot, and Blue.* Arthur Weinthal, a future CTV Network president, is writing supervisor. Somehow I think I can do better than what these guys are doing. So I quit and form my own revue group at Hillel Foundation.

Next year on campus, I produce *Squee-Dunk-U,* a very cheery, if unsophisticated, musical show, that satirizes everything that's happening on campus that year, and there's a lot happening. It's a hit. Another one, the following year—a prison show. (Don't ask me why.) Another hit. We're outdoing McGill's best musical shows. I don't really know what I'm doing, but somehow I'm doing it. I learn to write songs, first by parodying existing ones, then by composing simple original ones. Leonard Cohen sings one of mine—a prison song called "Closed-In Blues." I've written better songs since. So has Cohen. Quite a few. My best friend and co-music student, Howard Bacal, joins me in the process. He directs our shows while I produce them. Talented man, Howard. Goes on to become a renowned Beverly Hills psychiatrist. Could have been a great director. Or a great anything he wanted to be.

Producing is natural for me. Still is. Gives me a confidence that I never lose. And with this newfound self-assurance, I try debating again. Surprise! Leonard Cohen and I win the Inter-faculty Debating Cup. Imagine! The resolution is that "Canada be given back to the Indians." Not a bad idea. Ahead of its time. The debate blisters with humor. Cohen's opening address: "Ladies and gentlemen—I am not here to pluck another forensic feather for my ill-plumed cap!"

And you thought he was just another pretty face. I'm not bad either. Do my whole opening address in Latin, quoting from a book: *"Quid quid id est timeo Danaos et dona ferentes."*

I slam the book shut and don't bother to translate. Which makes it tough to refute, since neither of my opponents is fluent in Latin.

But theater is my passion. All in all, I produce and co-write eleven shows at McGill. Win a bunch of awards for them. And when the reporter from the college newspaper interviews me, she assumes that theater will be in my future.

"Theater?" I exclaim. "When I graduate? You gotta be kidding."

"No, why?"

"How am I gonna make a living doing that?" Good point, Rothman.

SO LIFE IS pretty frantic on campus. Between debating and producing, and a fast-paced social life (there are always pretty girls in my shows—but I'm sure you figured that out). Plus I'm still dating Lenore and Diana, my two high school sweethearts, who've now become my friends. I struggle to get through my college exams. Thank heavens, everything depends on our finals. I learn how to cram and pass exams, and somehow I graduate by the skin of my teeth.

{ 3 }

WELCOME

TO THE

REAL WORLD

*B*Y THE TIME I GRADUATE FROM
college, Dad has phased himself out
of dress manufacturing and bought an extensive textile mill
in the nearby lakeside town of Magog—a couple of hundred looms that weave cotton, wool, and linen fabrics for
the pants and dress trades, a dozen or so rapid-fire tricot
machines that knit synthetic fabrics (nylon, Dacron, rayon
blends) for the lingerie and blouse trades. Turns out a lot of
piece goods. Dad wants textiles for me because he thinks
it's a far more stable business than manufacturing dresses.
Doesn't want me in a crazy business. Ha!

So here I am in Dad's showroom, just graduated from
McGill with a degree in business. My father's proud of me.
"The secret of success in business—low overhead," he tells
me. He practices what he preaches—doesn't have an office.
That's why we're sitting in his showroom.

He comes from poverty—a small town in Poland—landed
in Canada, knowing nobody. He's a millionaire by the time
he's twenty-seven. When a million was a million. "It's no big

deal," he says. "I buy an item for five cents—I sell it for ten cents—I'm making my five percent, I'm happy." Yeah, Dad.

What a smart man he is. He makes his money during the Depression, bringing out stylish dresses for low prices. He has a great eye for style and a knack for making things inexpensively. It's an easy business to get into—doesn't take much capital—and in a short time he has a big business. Pretty soon he's rich. Then he builds apartment buildings and watches his capital gain. One by one, he brings his family over—first his mother and father, then his brothers and sisters. He puts them all in business, does all this by himself. And now, finally, he has his son, his younger son, his salesman son, to help him build an empire. And, in time, I'll take over.

"This is a proud day for me, my son," he says. "You, a college graduate, bringing all your knowledge into the business." He's smoking one of his three-for-a-quarter White Owl cigars. Won't smoke expensive ones—says they're too strong.

"But, Dad—you're the one who knows about business— I've got to learn from you."

He chuckles. "Sure, you'll learn from me, I'll learn from you... we'll learn from each other." He's perusing *Women's Wear Daily.* "Like this?" he says, holding up a picture of a high-style blouse. "Made of Dacron—DuPont's latest yarn— perfect for blouses, blended with cotton. What do you think, partner?"

"Dad, be serious, I want to learn. There must be certain business principles that made you successful. Tell me about them."

"Yes, my son, you're right, I can think of two." He puts down the magazine and gets serious. "The first principle is this: your word is your bond—you've got to keep your promises—all of them. I remember times when it cost me tens of thousands of dollars, but keeping your promise is the first principle for success."

"What's the second?"

He puffs on his cigar, George Burns style: "Never make any promises!"

I DON'T HATE the textile business. But I don't love it, either. I'm selling for my dad, and I'm pretty good at it. But my father is a tough taskmaster, very demanding, and I fear I'll never be as good as he is. True, there's fun to be had, lots of colorful characters in the business. People seem to like me and buy from me. I especially like the Syrian lingerie manufacturers. They're gentlemen.

"How can you do business with those people?" my father wants to know. "They're always polite to you, but you never know if they're going to buy."

"As opposed to *your* friends, the dress manufacturers. They're *never* polite, whether they're buying or not."

I prefer the Syrians. There are four families who manufacture 70 percent of Canada's lingerie. They're civilized and friendly, very easy to do business with. On one occasion I sell them enough fabric to make 144,000 panties, a record sale for our firm. After that, my father doesn't mind the Syrians so much.

One morning my father hands me a new fabric: sheer nylon net embossed with a flowered velvet pattern. Pretty. "Here," he says, "take this to your friend Jack Aberman at Rainbow Dress."

"He's not my friend, he's yours. He's a despicable man. We've never done business with him, and we never will."

"He'll buy this. I know his line—it's perfect for him. Tell him I'll give him for three months exclusive. He'll make millions." I pack the sample in my briefcase and leave.

Rainbow Dress is Canada's biggest ladies' formal wear manufacturer. Jack Aberman, its feisty, wily, mustachioed owner, is in the stockroom, sorting dresses by sizes and colors on various racks. He makes it a point never to look up when I enter the room.

"Mr. Aberman, can you spare a minute? I've got something to show you."

Not looking up, still sorting dresses, "Yes, Junior, what can I do for you."

"Mr. Aberman, it's a new cloth. My father wants you to see it first. Says it's perfect for your line and he'll give you a three months' exclusive."

Aberman, still sorting dresses: "Just leave it on the counter, Junior. I'll look at it later." Goes on sorting.

"Please, Mr. Aberman, give me two minutes. Dad knows your line. This is a new cloth, and he says you'll make a million on it."

This stops Jack Aberman in his tracks. He stops his sorting, comes to the counter, and rubs the material in six different directions. Then ponders.

"This cloth," he says very studiously, "is better than money."

Wow! Am I hearing right?

"You see, Junior, if it was money, I'd just spend it. Right away. But this cloth I'll have on my shelf for a lifetime. I'll never get rid of it!" he says, and goes back to sorting dresses.

WHEN I GET back to the office, there's a message to call Aberman.

"Listen," he whines, "maybe it's not such a bad cloth. Send me over nine yards of each color. I'll make up samples. How much you asking?"

"Two-forty a yard," I tell him.

"Ten percent discount," he demands, "or cancel my order. When will I get it?"

"Three days," I tell him. "You'll have it Friday."

Next morning, another call: "Junior, Jack Aberman, Rainbow Dress."

"Yes, Mr. Aberman."

"So where's my goods?"

"I told you Friday, Mr. Aberman, it's only Wednesday."

"So, you always have to wait till the last minute?"

Tough man. But my father is tougher. And smarter. He is right about the fabric—Aberman makes a fortune on it. So do we.

I'M TWENTY-TWO THE night I break the old man's heart. I come home from horseback riding and bring a friend with me. A friend my dad doesn't like. Never knew why. Syd is a nice guy, pleasant enough, a little rough-hewn maybe, not especially bright, but honestly, harmless. And we aren't that close. But we keep our horses at the same stable and enjoy riding together. After Syd leaves, my father calls me in. He's in the den, reading the paper.

"I told you I don't like this boy," he says, peering over the paper.

"Well, what is it you don't like about him, Dad?"

"I just don't like him, I have a feeling..."

"A feeling isn't enough, Dad, you've got to have a reason."

He lowers the paper and raises his voice. "My feeling is enough! I don't want to see him in this house again!"

"Too bad, but it's my house, too."

"No, it's not. And I don't want to see him here!"

"Then you won't see me, either!"

I storm out, slamming the door behind me. Climbing the circular staircase to my room, I am smoldering with resentment. It's probably been brewing inside me for a long time. It was always taken for granted I'd be in my dad's business. Nobody ever asked me. Mel could be a doctor or a lawyer or anything he pleased. My sister, Renee, could get married, do anything she wanted with her life. I never begrudged my siblings doing what they wanted. But I *had* to be in my dad's business. Why?

I hurry back down the stairs and burst into the den. My father is still reading the paper, and I don't give him time to lower it.

"I'm not coming to the office tomorrow, Dad. Or ever again! I'm through with your business!" And I storm back out.

I DON'T KNOW how long I wandered in that psychic wasteland. Maybe a month or two or three. It seems like forever. I know I hurt my dad, but I have a right to live my own life, and I'm not going to live it under his shadow. I'm looking for my next move. Maybe it's in advertising, maybe in business, maybe anything but show business. My father has relentlessly drilled into me that theater is not an option—it's not a legitimate business. And yet it's the only thing I've ever felt confident in.

My mother doesn't share my father's views. She loves the way I play the piano, feels I have talent, encourages me to follow my heart. Theater! But Montreal is a French city, doesn't have much English-speaking theater to offer. I remain hopelessly confused. Coming home every evening means putting up with my father's taunts of the "You'll never amount to anything" variety. Then, I overhear my mother and my father fighting in their bedroom over me:

"We never should have sent him to college! That's where he got those fancy ideas!"

"They're not fancy ideas, Charlie. He's entitled to choose what he wants. You did. And you made a success of it. But not everyone needs to make millions."

My father raises his voice: "I didn't build up a business for my family to throw away, Nellie. Somebody has to take over—I'm getting old!"

"He's got to use his talent. It's the best part of him," says my mother. "He can't waste himself in a business he doesn't like. If you'd done that, you'd still be in Poland."

Don't know what to do. So I go back to the scene of the crime—McGill.

Dr. Solin is the dean of Business Studies, and I remember him as a very special, very practical man. I didn't know him well, but I knew him.

"You're probably wondering why I've come to see you, Dr. Solin."

"Let me guess," he says. "You've left your dad's business and broken his heart."

"Yes, I have." How does he know? He doesn't know my dad.

"Happens all the time. I remember reading an interview with you in the school paper. You surprised me by saying you were joining your dad's business. I couldn't figure out why—you'd done amazing work on our shows here."

"It's just that it was expected of me—I never thought much about it."

"I don't know why fathers expect their sons to follow in

their footsteps. You were brought up differently, different economic circumstances—you're different people."

"My father is a great businessman—brilliant! I could never be as good as he is."

"But I'll bet you're a much better writer. And producer. So why not give yourself a chance? Follow your heart."

I leave Dean Solin's office more confused than ever. Can I really have a career in theater? How? Where? It's the first time I've allowed myself the luxury of these feelings.

I go to see Stephen Porter. Stephen is a young professor at McGill, out of the Yale School of Drama. I'd learned enormously from his classes.

"What are you doing in these hallowed halls?" he asks me, his tongue firmly placed in the dramatic side of his cheek. I had been one of his favorite students, and I was sure he knew why I was there.

"I've left my father's business, Stephen, and I'm considering a career in theater."

"You're *considering* theater?" he said. "You're *considering* it? What's to consider—you'll do brilliantly." Veddy, veddy dramatic, Stephen, but he's just what I need.

Actually, it's Stephen who's brilliant. He soon goes on to an amazing career, directing plays on Broadway and at the repertory theater in San Francisco. But his words stick in my mind—over and over. Maybe, just maybe, I can pull it off.

THE FINAL IMPETUS comes from my brother, Mel, after dinner that night. We were watching Percy Saltzman do the weather on *Tabloid,* an early magazine-show hit on Canadian television. I tell Mel about my meetings with Dr. Solin and Stephen Porter.

"Well? What are you going to do, Bernie?"

"I just don't know. There's so little theater in this city."

"So try another city."

"Where, Mel? I hate New York."

"How 'bout Toronto?"

"What's in Toronto?"

"Television, Bernie, there's television in Toronto."

"I hate television, you know that. It's so—so lowbrow."

"Ridiculous! There's all kinds of stuff in television. Most important, there's jobs! Why don't you go and get one?"

"Hmm, maybe. I'll think about it."

Of course he's right—a job is what I need. If I can support myself, I'll be free from all my father's bossing around, free to do what I want with my life. Don't get me wrong—my father was a good man. No, a great man. Possibly the smartest man I ever met. I don't want to disappoint him. But Dean Solin is right. We're different people—with different sensibilities. My father is a business genius—I'm not. Maybe I can do something with my life that's just as important and feel good about myself.

I make up my mind—I'll go get a job as a TV producer. I know guys with a lot less talent than I have who got in the TV game. So that's it—I'm outta here!

Next day, I start a journey that will change my life forever. With a little help from my friends, of course.

4

THE

RUNAWAY

"*M*ERV ROSENZWEIG THINKS THE world of you, Bernie. Did you pay him or something?"

"We went to college together. Merv worked on the school paper; I produced shows."

"And great ones, he tells me. Says you're very talented."

"Said nice things about you, too. Figured maybe you could help."

I'm talking to Len Starmer, CBC's deputy chief of Variety Television, the music and comedy world. Len's a very affable man, makes me feel right at home. Mid-forties, silver haired, tall and slender, Len moves like a dancer, which he had once been. He interviews me in his modest office in Toronto. It's little more than a cubicle. "The Corp" has taken over an abandoned high school, and the Variety department occupies an entire floor. You would have described it as threadbare but for the fact that the walls are covered with free-style cartoons, scrawled by the late George Feyer, a very talented caricaturist. It's a colorful place. But the Canadian

Broadcasting Corporation is government owned and can't spend freely. It will be years before they build a central complex. Meanwhile, they house their various departments in dilapidated buildings all over the city.

This interview is a big deal for me. I'm all of twenty-two, floundering, and broke. Well, not quite broke. I have four hundred dollars left over from my bar mitzvah money. But unless I can figure out a way for that to last the rest of my life, I'll be back in textiles, a prospect as pleasurable as a case of shingles. I need a job.

"So how can I get you started, young man?" Len asks, smiling.

I smile right back. "How about a producer's job?"

Len laughs. "You *are* a bit cheeky," he says, "and I like that. But I can't start you at the top."

"Why not try?" I say, feigning disappointment.

Len ignores this and goes on. "We have a position we call studio director. It's a combination of stage manager and assistant to the producer. Great way for you to break in. Learn and grow. Doesn't pay too well—you'll have a tough time making ends meet—unless your father happens to be a millionaire..."

"Well, actually, he is, Len..."

Len yelps like a puppy dog. Apparently, it's a stock speech he gives to all prospective studio directors. I'm the only one who ever called him on it.

"When do I start?" the cheeky me asks.

"Can't hire you right away, Bern. But maybe in the fall. Call me in August—I think you'll do great here."

Studio director? Stage manager? Sounds good! Does he mean it? Or is he just another slick bureaucrat? Seems to like me... but August is an eternity away. I desperately need something sooner or I won't survive. Back to Dad's business? Never, never, never!

IT'S STAN JACOBSON who steers me to the Centre Island Playhouse, a charming little summer theater that saves my life. He and his producing partner, the aforementioned Merv Rosenzweig, had checked it out the summer before but latterly fell into the resort-based Red Barn Theatre, which, unlike the Centre Island facility, needed no fixing up.

Merv is a CBC producer, does interviews with celebrities for a magazine show. He and Jacobson share a nouveau-ish apartment in the center of town. Merv brings me home to meet his stage-producing partner, a big, burly guy, who only talks when his mouth is full of food and can't have a conversation unless the TV is on full blast. Jacobson, who's made a bundle of money selling aluminum siding, loves theater and turns out to be an excellent producer, in spite of his table manners.

Both boys have creative aspirations, and they've produced a solid season of summer plays. Sure, they lost a few bucks. But they've made a name for themselves in the Toronto theater community, and they're able to raise the money they need to produce major plays in downtown Toronto. Which they've been doing. Boy, am I jealous!

I'm also grateful. The Centre Island Playhouse is just what I need to keep busy until that CBC opportunity opens up. And what a location for a summer theater—a ten-minute ferryboat ride from downtown Toronto, situated on a picturesque island in the middle of Lake Ontario. It's an old movie house, abandoned after a few years, because there just weren't enough residents on the island to make it pay. Still, I'm sure that on sunny summer evenings, they'll cross

Lake Ontario in droves to come see my plays. I'll just have to produce the right plays, and it's a shoo-in. Bye-bye Daddy's business forever! Yeah, right.

WHAT A BREAK! I hurry back to Montreal and start raising money. Figure I need ten thousand dollars—five thousand to build the stage, another five to get the theater company up and running. Easy!

I start with my Dad. I'm not too thrilled to go there, but I don't have much choice. And if I'm not thrilled, you can imagine how unthrilled my dad is. Gives me two thousand on condition that I never ask him for another nickel. Truthfully, I'm lucky to get anything, considering how I'd walked out on him. It's not that he doesn't believe in *me*. He just doesn't believe in "the business." He gives me the money under protest. I take it, with no protest at all.

My next stop is John Pratt. John is a well-known Montreal show business personality who directed a McGill revue for me. He is twenty years my senior, has been an actor, an architect, a Member of Parliament, and lovable man-around-town. Some see him as a scoundrel. I don't. He's kind, loyal, charming, and always good company. So okay, maybe John loves the ladies too well. Or too many of them. Big deal! I get John at the right time. His wife is divorcing him. He comes in with his two thousand, and I have a partner with a résumé. Remember—I'm twenty-two. I need someone with legitimate experience. John is perfect.

Next come my buddies—Joe and Nassie and Howard and Doug and Hank and Ted and Marvin and the others—they each pitch in a couple of hundred bucks. Just for the fun of it! And to show support, bless them.

Finally, there's Max Rothstein. Max is a wealthy business-man, the father of my best friend's fiancée. He's dying to help, and he does. I ask him for two and a half thousand; he throws in five. That's all I need, or so I believe. But another half-million wouldn't hurt.

So John and I move to Toronto. John is well known there and introduces me to the community. Being a Montrealer, I always looked down on this rather bland city. Can't get a drink after midnight. Can't see a movie on Sunday. But after being there a short time, I realize what a sophisticated city it is. Montreal is French, and English-speaking theater activity is very limited. Not so in Toronto. There are great art galleries that people actually attend. There is a beautiful concert hall with a first-rate symphony orchestra. There's a vibrant theater life, including a long-running musical revue, *Spring Thaw*. Very impressive. Its star is a handsome young man of French-Canadian extraction, with a great baritone voice. Robert Goulet was his name. Still is. For Bob I write a song that grabs a lot of attention in the next edition of *Spring Thaw*. It's about a tough French-Canadian motorcycle kid, rebelling against his elders and the *maudit anglais* (goddamn English) who are keeping him down. He sings:

I'm da boy in da black jaquette
And I don't give a damn for no one 'oo
Doesn't ride motor bicyclette
C'est moi—dat's me

Later, the lyrics take on a nasty Separatist turn:

Now in Ottawa dey said—we got nutting in da head
But dey all drop dead, every one of dem instead
When we t'row all de Inglishers out on dere neck
Well 'oo you t'ink gonna run Quebec???

Dat's da boys in da black jaquette . . . and so on . . .

Maclean's magazine publishes an excerpt of the lyrics as a sign of the times. It's the first song I ever got paid for. *Spring Thaw* paid me three dollars a performance (Canadian), twenty-one bucks a week. Wow!

In May, we take possession of the theater, and renovations begin. I live upstairs of a restaurant on Centre Island's main street. The smells make me crazy, but the work is fun. My college buddy Irwin Browns comes down from Montreal, and we paint the sets together, recover sofas together, read plays for upcoming productions. John interviews directors, hires actors, romances the leading ladies. We figure we need seven or eight plays for the summer season. Which means doing a new show every week, rehearsing another while the first is playing. I guess the frantic pace prepares me for the madness of weekly television. It doesn't leave much time for a social life.

The theater opens with a gala performance of *The Little Hut*, a British romantic comedy, starring three of Toronto's biggest stage stars. And a gorilla. The day before opening, I put on the gorilla suit, ride around downtown Toronto in the back of a Jeep, with a sign on my back that reads, "See me running wild on Centre Island." (For this I needed a college degree?) It's a hot day, and I swelter! A full house for opening night, and everything goes exactly as planned. *Except for the power failure.* I make a funny curtain speech, imploring the audience to be patient and get to know their neighbors. Then we play the whole second act by flashlight. Audience loves it!

Next day, the papers are full of it—great publicity. We pack 'em in all week. Same for the second week, for *Tender Trap,* another romantic comedy, super-good cast without a gorilla. Our audience is building. *Moon Is Blue* in our third week, best cast of all, great reviews—we're flying!

Soon we run out of plays. The good ones, I mean. And the good actors are getting expensive. We need light comedies with a small cast and a single, easy-to-build set. They're hard to come by. Then the rains start and really cook our goose. No one wants to cross the lake in bad weather. Of the next four plays, only one makes money. The other three lose more than we've made all season. As the audience enters, I peer through a slit in the backstage curtain, count the house, and hope that a vast crowd will miraculously show up at the last minute. But it doesn't. I need two hundred people to break even. Some weeknights I get less than eighty. Some matinees, those poor actors play to a dozen people. Pathetic! I'm losing my shirt. Mine and everyone else's. My first professional venture is a disaster. My dreams are going up in smoke.

So I pack my bag and run back to Montreal. I have to face my backers, tell them the news that I don't have a penny left. In fact, I'm a couple of thousand in the hole, and I have to think of a way to start paying back.

I face Max Rothstein first. He is not amused. He informs me that half the money he gave me was a loan, not an investment. News to me. But Max expects me to pay twenty-five hundred dollars back, and from the look on his face, he means it. The rumors that Max was "connected" spring to mind. Where the hell am I going to get that money? And what will happen to me if I don't? I have no job—I'm broke. I certainly can't ask my father for a loan, because the answer will be no. Everything I can think of is a dead end. My dream is over.

I drive home that night truly despondent. Luckily, there are no bridges to jump off on the way. I enter the house, tiptoe down the hall, careful not to wake my father as I pass his bedroom. The maid has left me a note on my desk, one of those pink phone message slips, dated four o'clock that afternoon: "A Mister Starmer, of CBC, Toronto, called."

"Hail Mary, Mother of Jesus," I say. Three times. Then I remind myself that I'm Jewish.

5

GETTING

MY FEET

WET IN TV

THE BEST DIRECTOR I EVER WORKED with was Norman Jewison. There were others—Glenn Jordan (a fine director of dramatic films), Stan Harris (a super visual director), Rob Iscove, and Ron Field—excellent directors who started as choreographers on Broadway—and Louis J. Horvitz, who does such a great job on the Oscars. But Norman was the best. He was also the first. He's twenty-eight when we first work together, and you can see the talent oozing out of him. A great storyteller, in person as well as on the screen, Jewison will go on to direct *Fiddler on the Roof, Moonstruck, In the Heat of the Night, The Hurricane, The Russians Are Coming, The Soldiers' Story,* and other excellent films too numerous to mention. Amazing!

Norman is my first boss in Canadian television; I'm his studio director—which is just a fancy term for a stage manager who helps his producer/director boss organize his show. Orders the props and sets and costumes and all the special effects that the script requires. Later Norman is my first boss in U.S. television; I'm one of his writers. In between, we work on a couple of stage shows together. He's always warm and welcoming, and more than anything, inclusive. Everybody's contributions are important to Norman, and he lets you know it. You can't help but like the man and, more important, learn from him.

He has this colorful personality, full of energy. I'm sure everyone has Jewison stories—I've got lots. But the one I'm going to tell you is about my very first day in a TV studio.

It's 1957 and I've just turned twenty-three when the CBC hires me as a studio director. Don't know why—it's a craft I know nothing about. The job is very complicated—I'm responsible for everything that happens on the studio floor. The show's director, who rehearses with the cast all week, spends most of his time in the control booth on studio days. Through their headsets, he can communicate with his camera-men, soundmen, lighting men, and yes, with me, his studio director. It's my job to take charge of the studio floor—get the actors into position, get the stagehands to change the sets, coordinate cast and crew so that each member of the team is ready to do his job at the right time. Silently! Because we're working in live television. Which means that anyone caught out of position might be seen on camera doing things we don't want the home viewers to see. Like changing the set, for instance. All this is difficult for me. Confusing. Remember—I've never set foot in a TV studio before that day. Scary, very scary. But I'm desperate enough to try anything. I've already screwed up my career in theater; I can't afford a failure in TV.

After two or three days of orientation—learning critical stuff, like how to fill out my time card, what the best pizza flavor is in the cafeteria—they send me over to the studio to meet my new boss. Love at first sight! He makes me feel I am,

if anything, overqualified for the job, that he's been waiting his whole career for someone as talented as I am to come
along and show him how to produce shows. Figure it's a bit
of a stretch, but I'm thrilled to be on board with a captain
who so reveres his crew.

Norman hands me over to Peter Scott, the experienced
studio director, who, in time, I'm going to replace.

"Get a headset on, and follow Peter around," Norman tells
me. "Nobody better to show you the ropes."

Rehearsals for a live TV show. What fun! With my ear-
phones on, I can hear Norman up in the control booth bark-
ing out orders to his cameramen—"Ready two on Alex, in
five-four-three-two-one, take two, cue Alex," Alex being
Alex Barris, the show's host. I watch Peter Scott as he stands
beside a camera, flexes his arm like a tennis player, then
throws a cue to Alex like he's throwing a baseball at him.
But without the ball. Exciting! And when they roll in a pre-
filmed commercial, Peter supervises the stagehands, who,
like a team of soldier ants, make rapid changes in the scenery. He coordinates all this, calling out at intervals how
much time is left to the commercial—"Thirty seconds!"—so
that when the show is back on the air live, the scenery is in
place and no one is caught on camera. "Five-four-three-two-
one—cue Alex!" Magic!

Throughout the rehearsal, people are relaxed, friendly.
But I know the show is being carefully rehearsed for the
moment of truth—ten o'clock that night, they'll be on the
air, live. Happily, I'll be home in bed, watching the broadcast, while poor Peter Scott, the show's real stage manager,
will be managing the stage. Tough job. I wonder how soon
I'll be ready to take over. Two weeks? A month? A couple
of months?

Dinner break at 7:00 PM. "How ya doin'?" Norman wants to know. "*You* tell *me*," I reply. "Let's see," he says, and counts me down: "In five-four-three-two-one, cue Alex." I throw the cue the way I saw Peter do it. "That's great," he says. "You learn fast. How about you stage-manage the 'dress'?"

"Oh, I don't know, Norman, you think I'm..."

"Ready? 'Course I do. Hey—it's just a rehearsal."

So I stage-manage the "dress." No, that's an exaggeration. What I do is watch the dress rehearsal stage-manage itself. And I join the party once in a while for "five-four-three-two-one, cue Alex." Believe me, I'm relieved to take off my headset when it's over, knowing I have a lot to learn.

I look around to find Peter, thank him for his kindness. Can't find him. Look everywhere; he's nowhere. Then someone says, "I think he went home," and I'm in a panic. Ten minutes to air time, and no stage manager! I tear up the stairs to the control booth, and there's Norman, halfway up, smiling at me.

"Norman—I can't find Peter! I was just about to leave, and..."

"Oh, don't do that, Bernie, we need you." He is annoyingly calm.

"But where's Peter?"

"I sent him home."

"You what? Who's gonna stage-manage?"

"Well, I can't. I've gotta direct. So I guess it's *you*."

"What? You want me to stage-manage a live show—first day in the studio?"

"Why not? You can do it. There's such a thing as too much training, you know."

"You're crazy, Norman."

"You're not the first person to tell me that. And doubtless, there'll be others. Now get out there and do your 'five-four-three-two-one, cue Alex' routine."

And I did. Somehow, I did. Terrified, I did. Nothing in television ever scared me again.

I NEVER FELT so good in my life. No homework, no piano lessons, no family to boss me around—I'm free. Really free!

I share a studio apartment with an actor friend. Sleep in a pull-out Murphy bed, in a tacky 10 × 15 room, decorated in early orange crate, located in the heart of Toronto's red-light district. This red light needs its bulb changed. The building has to be totally remodeled before the city will condemn it. But to me, it's the Taj Mahal. I love living there. Come home every night, cook a sumptuous meal of wieners and beans. Go to the movies, get home just in time to see the taverns empty out, sleep like a baby through the moans and cries of the sex scene going on next door. It's an adventure for me. I'm taking home fifty-seven bucks a week, and I love my life. Because it's mine!

Meanwhile, I'm learning a great deal about television at the CBC.

I learn that you can't do a moving shot on a long lens without losing focus.

And you'd better avoid a wide-angle lens on your close-up, or you're likely to give your leading lady a big nose.

If they ask you for a montage, they mean a series of quick shots, usually based on a central theme or sequence, often set to music, edited together so that each shot comes on a musical beat.

A principal actor may get paid $300 for a show, for which he or she will rehearse eight hours. A bit player gets $150, speaks no more than six lines, and gives you four hours of rehearsal for that. A super (or extra) gets $100, can speak no lines, and can only take group direction from the assistant director.

Over the years, you pick up a lot of detail, all useful, all critical. It's your job to know all this stuff. Especially if you're planning to be a producer.

While I'm stage-managing at the CBC, learning about television, earning my independence, CBC gives me time off to pursue my first love—producing live stage revues. There are two notable ones.

The first, called *Off Limits,* plays Montreal's cozy Mountain Playhouse. Great cast—the brilliant Jack Creley, comic Dave Broadfoot (Canada's first real stand-up), and a versatile ensemble of sketch players. By now I know who the top TV writers are. I go after them, whet their appetites to create something exciting for the stage. And we do.

Norman Jewison directs it—magnificently. Announced for a two-week run, it gets rave reviews and runs for twelve. The backers make money; I don't. I've given away everything just to raise the capital. But now that I know the secret formula, it'll be easy to do it again.

Next year I do another: same super group of writers— Frank Peppiatt, John Aylesworth, Saul Ilson, Allan Manings, Ray Jessel, Norman Sedawie, Alex Barris, (we all end up in Hollywood a few years later)—again to be directed by Jewison. Norman is already working in the States, but *Off Limits* was such a triumph, he comes back to direct *After Hours.* Same cast, essentially, but we add three fine singers in Betty Robertson, Don Francks, and Allan Blye. We also have more money for sets and costumes. How could we miss?

We open again at the Mountain Playhouse, then, after a six-week run, move on to the Stratford Festival. This is a big deal. No outside production has ever been commissioned by the festival. The press gives us a lot of space. I'm confident my career will be made. It's not.

The critics pan *After Hours,* and they're right to. The material isn't as good; the cast is talented, but the chemistry isn't the same. We have to close the show early. Once again, I lose my paltry little shirt. Takes me two years to pay it off. Will I ever learn?

Answer: yes! I make the decision to never again produce a stage play.

And I never do.

6

ONWARD

AND

UPWARD

*S*O OKAY, I'M LIVING IN TORONTO earning a big eighty-five dollars a week, stage-managing at the CBC, loving living on my own. Thrilled not to be in Montreal, where everybody knows me, knows my family, expects things of me. In Toronto nobody knows me or expects anything. But I'm on my own. No social life, no cultural structure; nobody introduces me to anyone. In short, I've got show business, but that's all.

I go out with Babs Tasherean, a tall, long-legged show dancer. Nice girl, but we don't have much to talk about. Invite her and Dave Broadfoot over, hoping to impress her by cooking a sumptuous gourmet dinner. When I take her home after dinner, she gives me a long, languid, sexy kiss on her doorstep. My eyes are still closed as I hear her say, "Gee, Bernie—you're a swell cook!" And she disappears through the door before I can get my eyes open.

This is not my idea of an intimate evening. There are other evenings like it—not my glass of tea. So I don't go out much.

Then, a call from a young woman I knew slightly in Montreal. Patricia Harris, a McGill girl from an English family, who'd gone to Yale Drama and gotten herself married to a guy from Texas. (Talk about cross-culturalization!) She's an actress, working at a small theater in Boston, and has come up to audition for the Stratford people. The marriage is just about over, so we date. And although she doesn't get the part with the Shakespearean company, she stays in Toronto, and a year later, we're living together.

It's a comfortable relationship. We have lots in common—friends, Montreal, a passion for the theater, gourmet cooking—lots. We get married a year later in Montreal at the Ritz-Carlton Hotel with a glitzy wedding she plans with my parents—a couple hundred guests. I arrive from work in Toronto the day before, and honestly, I have no idea who's coming to the wedding. I'm in such a daze, I'm not even sure if *I'm* at the wedding! A week's honeymoon in Mexico, then back to Toronto, where we settle into domestic bliss (ha!) in a cozy cottage on someone's country estate on the outskirts of the city. Just Trish and me and a three-year-old stallion named Tonto.

It's all very dreamlike, but then, we're used to that. The spine of my life remains my job in TV. They give me a raise, so I'm now getting an opulent hundred and fifteen dollars a week—plenty for newlyweds to live on. After all, we have no kids.

Trish becomes pregnant, and now I've got to get serious about this money thing. Time to focus on my career—move up to the next level. I've allowed the personal part of my life to take over; I've neglected my career, put my goal of producing on the back burner. Common sense tells me if I don't push myself, nobody else will. So I become both the "pusher" and the "pushee." I know I can produce, and so does everybody I've ever worked with. But I need a break. And the Canadian Broadcasting Corporation, a government agency, moves at a snail's pace—maybe slower. I wonder—will they ever give me a break?

They never do. Not really. It's my friend Murray Chercover who helps me break out of stage managers' prison. CTV, Canada's new commercial network, has hired Murray as program director for its flagship station. He's an excellent producer himself and a very knowledgeable television executive. (He soon becomes CTV's president, a position he holds for twenty-three years.) We had worked together at CBC, become friends over the years, and when he calls to offer me my own series to direct, I feel like I've been freed from bondage. Fabulous!

I march right into Starmer's office, thank him for years of support, and fire the CBC.

Len can't believe his ears. How can I do this to them? Leave now, knowing all their hopes for me?

"Len," I say, "I gotta look after my family. Can't do it on a hundred and fifteen bucks a week!"

That gets to him. Len is a family man himself, and he cares about me. "Gimme a day or two," he implores. "See if I can come up with something."

What he comes up with is a writer's job. On CBC's prestigious *Jack Kane Show*. A big-band series—the best I've ever seen—with great comedy elements, big-name guest stars, and big-band music that's exciting and telegenic. I'm disappointed not to be getting a producing job. But the money is three times what I've been making, and it's a full season's contract. Me! A big-time TV writer! Wow! This is much better than CTV's offer. Oh sure, the contract will run out after a year. But I'll take care of Trish and the baby this year and worry about next year, next year.

Then, a scary question twists and turns in my mind: *can I actually write?* Every day? Oh, sure—I've written songs, sketches—done it since college days. But this is different. Writing every day. Sitting down at a typewriter at nine thirty in the morning. Staying there till dinnertime. Pages and pages, every day, five days a week, week after week, month after month. Can I do it?

I need a second opinion.

"SURE YOU CAN write, Bern," says Frank Peppiatt, dean of the Canadian TV writers. We're at the bar at Bassel's Restaurant, a crowded hangout, where we can barely hear each other talk.

Frank orders another martini. "A little drier with this one, pal," he says to the waiter. Then to me: "Think I would have recommended you if I didn't feel you could do the job?"

Is he lying? Did he really recommend me? If he did, why didn't Len tell me? And if he didn't, how can I believe anything else he says?

Frank and I had worked well together on a number of shows. He's a brilliant TV veteran, and I've learned a lot from him. At a hulking six foot four, he tends to bend the truth a bit when he drinks. And he *does* drink.

"Look, I know I can write, Frank. But do you think I can do it for a living?"

"Sure, why not? You got the talent," he says, carefully spearing the olive. "The rest is just practice." He throws back the martini in a gulp.

"What d'ya mean, 'practice'?" I ask.

"You know—practice. It's like anything else. The more you do it, the better you get. Sit down with a pad and pencil every day—you should write something every single day. Seven days a week!"

Is he kidding? I can't write seven days a week. I'm not even sure I can write five.

"Not kidding, Bern. See, the hardest thing about writing is getting started. A writer's worst enemy is the blank page. So, just sit down, and throw some stuff up there. And don't be critical. Till the next day. Then you can rewrite. Rewriting is much easier than writing. And rewriting is what makes the writing good."

By now, Frank has finished his fourth martini, and he's balancing the glass on his forehead like a trained seal. "Am I making any sense?" he asks, as I grab the glass and set it down on the table.

"Perfect sense," I lie, as the waiter pours Frank his next drink without even asking. They know him here.

"Oh, and one more thing," he says, suddenly serious. "Don't get too involved with the words."

"What?"

"The words—they're not important. Don't waste your time on them. It's the ideas that count. And you've got good ones."

He throws back the last of his drink and gets up, empty glass in hand.

"You'll be one of the greats, Bern. If you stick with it."

"Thanks, Frank."

"But I have the feeling writing's just a stepping-stone for you—you want to produce, don't you?

"Yeah, eventually."

"Learn to write first," he says. "You'll never regret it." He bumps his head on the door on the way out.

I learned to write. And I've never regretted it.

SO WHAT IS this writing stuff all about?

Well, at first I only write what I want to write. And that's easy. I can get up in the middle of the night with an inspiration and spend the whole night working on it. I do that on a revue song for *Off Limits*. Got an idea about two leprechauns doing a song and dance about how things have changed on the Emerald Isle—

> *Things have changed a little bit in Ireland*
> *Things are not like what they were before*
> *Things have changed a little bit in Ireland*
> *They're not the same at drinkin' anymore*
> *For many years the little dears*
> *Left nothin' much to waste*
> *Distillin' Irish Whisky*
> *With a truly Irish taste*
> *But when the man from Seagram's came*
> *The taste was all replaced*
> *Oh, you'll never recognize*
> *You'll not believe yer eyes*
> *You'll never recognize the darlin' place!*

Wrote it in an hour. It was the highlight of the revue.

But this is different. I'm working for a producer—okay, it's Stan Harris, and we get along well. And I'm writing dialogue for performers—have to tailor the words to fit the sound of their voices. I know Jack Kane and the characters on the show, but it isn't easy to do good comic dialogue in their cadence. Good jokes are hard enough to write, but it has to sound as if the people saying them are making them up as they go along. And what about the guest stars? Some I know; some I don't. Jack Benny is easy to write for. He has a special pattern of talking, special words he likes to use—like "gosh," and "well!" And you'd always score by writing jokes about his vanity. Jackie Mason is easy to write for. New York, Jewish. Very specific. Bill Cosby's a snap. Just write for his drawl.

But even when you get their speech pattern, there's never

enough time to perfect their lines. It's my first *Jack Kane Show,* and Andy Williams is guest star. I've written a pretty decent script, and he's doing it just fine. But after dress rehearsal, Andy comes over and sez, "Hey, kid—I need some new jokes for that spot with the band."

"Sure, Andy. How many?"

"Well, there's the brass and the reeds—figure eight or ten."

Gulp! I have twenty minutes to write them. I tell Andy I'll be right back. Then, I disappear into the bathroom and never show up again. The show goes on with Andy doing the old gags, and it's just fine. But an experienced writer could do what Andy asked in a flash. I'm just not that experienced a writer. And I don't have the confidence that comes with experience. Confidence means everything to a writer.

If you don't think you can write it, you probably can't. The great Italian playwright Luigi Pirandello (*Six Characters in Search of an Author*) phrased it better in the title of a play: *Right You Are If You Think You Are.* That's what the great playwright wrote.

And I think the playwright wrote right.

7

WALTZING

MATHILDA

*A*T THE END OF MY FIRST FULL SEASON as a TV writer in Canada, I'm out of work and feeling shaky. My contract has run out, and although I've saved a few pennies, with my wife about to give birth to our second child, I'd better get looking.

I canvass every producer I know. Nothing available. Was my first writing job my last? Was my father right—I would never have a secure life unless I come back to his business? After five years of struggling in show business, am I doomed to surrender? Surely I can do something. Custer made a last stand; why can't I? Well, there was a last stand to be made, but I had to leave the country to make it.

It's 1961. MCA, the holding company for Universal Studios, is packaging a big, splashy variety series in Australia, the country's first. Peter MacFarlane, the Canadian producer-director, is looking for someone to "head-write" it but can't afford one of those high-priced head writers. With the help of my friend and CBC writing colleague Saul Ilson, we persuade Peter that even a single season's Canadian experience is enough for me to teach those Aussies how to write. Saul, who knows Peter well, sends him a telegram: "Highly recommend Rothman as the best of the cheaper writers." I'm waiting for an answer like my life depends on it. Because it does.

Peter's special-delivery offer comes as my wife is about to make her own special delivery. Between contractions I ask her how she would feel about my taking a job in Australia.

"I'll miss you very much," she says.

"No, dear, we're all going to live in Sydney for a while. And the money's good," I say.

"Super!" she says. "I like it when the money's good." She winces. "How long?" she asks.

"Six months firm. But Peter says we can stay longer if it suits us," I tell her.

Trish says, "Is there running water and electricity where we're going?"

"Of course," I answer.

Big contraction. "Then it suits us," she says. "Now go away and let me have this baby!"

Groan.

WE LAND IN Sydney three weeks later on a Saturday. The trip with our two little ones has been horrendous. But the taxi ride to the hotel gives us a panoramic view of the most beautiful city we've ever seen. Beaches that make Waikiki look like a sandbox. A bustling city that reminds you of downtown London. The Kings Cross district is as bohemian as Soho, with twice the charm. And that bridge—the Sydney Harbour Bridge—breathtaking! So already we love it.

Next day, I go out looking for an apartment. I find a cab driver who not only drives me, but he also tells me where to look. We spend half the day together, and I rent this charming coach house in Darling Point, Sydney's beautiful embassy district. The meter, for half a day's travel, reads thirty-seven pounds, thirteen shillings, and two pence. And the driver says to me, "Make it thirty-five even, right mate?"

How d'ya like that? *He's* tipping *me!*

Basically, there's no tipping in Australia. Why? Because there's no class system. You never hear anyone brag that his family came over on the *Mayflower,* because most of the first Australians were convicts. I love the fact that in the pubs you'll meet bosses drinking with their secretaries, neurosurgeons with garbage collectors—maybe they're strange bedfellows, but it works. People learn about each other, get along better because of it. They work hard to earn enough—not to elevate their social stature, but to enjoy their lives. And nobody is better at enjoyment than the Australians. We have a lot to learn from these people and the way they live. And by the way, they clearly love North Americans. Maybe because their lifestyle is similar to ours. They may sound like Brits to untrained ears, but they're far from British in their makeup. And proud of it.

DIGBY WOLFE IS the show's compere (MC). And he's excellent. A handsome, elegant man in his forties, he hails from England, where he achieved semisuccess as an acerbic stand-up. He wanted to be Lenny Bruce. Bad casting. Much too suave, too well spoken. But as the witty front man of a beautifully packaged variety series, he's perfect. He makes Ed Sullivan look like an amateur.

This is already an extremely successful venture. Looking at the show, I wonder why Peter thinks he needs me. It's a booker's show, meaning its success depends mostly on the guest stars you book. So I work on structuring the show, changing the format, giving it connective tissue and continuity. The short in-between bits that help give the show pace.

We book Johnny Lockwood, a delightful cockney baggy-pants comic, as Digby's adoring sidekick. He's straight out of the music hall.

"I'm 'ere," says Johnny slyly, as he sneaks up behind Digby in the middle of his monologue. The audience sees the funny little man first, begins tittering. Johnny stands behind Digby, staring at him in adulation. Digby scowls.

"Go right on, mate," Johnny says. "Pay no attention. I just wanna watch the master do 'is job!" Well, of course Digby can't.

"Go on, mate," says Johnny. "You're amazing! So smooth, so suave, so devilishly handsome!" By now the audience is hysterical.

We do nostalgic music segments based on everyone's favorite love song, dating all the way back to Stephen Foster. The twenty-member choir sings magnificently. And looks great, too.

We do guy talk, a humorous conversation Digby has with his American male guest star, as they satirize U.S. politics, shooting pool around a billiard table. And on and on...

It's a great group to work with. Peter is very supportive, the show has a brilliant comedy writer in Chris Beard, and Digby is always willing to take a chance on new material. He's also willing to throw out the entire opening monologue twenty minutes before showtime.

"It's not working, chum," says Digby in clipped British tones. "You can't do an American political monologue on Australian television. They won't understand it, and it's got to go!"

"Okay," I say, " and replace it with..."

"A new one," says Digby, smiling. "About Australian politics."

"Digby, are you nuts? We're ten minutes away from letting the audience in."

"Oh, you'll come up with something."

And we do. An old one out of Chris Beard's trunk.

I think I added dimensions to the show. But I also learned a great deal. Digby and Chris come up with the wildest ideas for the show. Broad comedy, like silent movie stuff, chase sequences, slapstick—it all works. Ten years later both those men show up in Hollywood, two of the original creators of *Laugh-In*.

AFTER SIX WEEKS, Peter takes me out to an elegant dinner. Wants to talk. He's a nice man, talented, fun to work with and a real straight shooter. We're on our dessert.

"You getting along all right?" he asks.

"Loving it," I say.

"What about the family—anything we can do to make them more comfortable?"

"Peter, you've done everything we could ask for and more. And that nanny they got us is terrific!"

"Good. Because I love what you're doing here. You've made the writers into a real unit, and I feel much more secure about the creative arm of the show."

"Thanks. This trip is such an eye-opener. I always thought Australia was the end of the earth, the boonies. But it's a great place to work, to bring up a family!"

"I'm glad you feel that way, Bernie."

He leans in, rubbing the rim of his cognac snifter. I know what's coming, and I dread it.

"I want you to stay on. Past your six-month commitment.

I talked to the brass. They're willing to give you a big bump in salary. On a two-year deal."

"Peter, I did a stupid thing before I left. CBC got wind I was leaving and offered me a deal to come back."

Peter is crushed. Argh!

"I shouldn't have done it. But coming here was taking a plunge into darkness. I didn't have the guts to turn Canada down."

"Any chance you can delay that deal?"

"No. But I can break it."

He's shocked. I continue: "I'll break it if..."

Now I got him. "If what?"

Now it's my turn for rhetoric. "Peter, you're the producer of the biggest hit in this country's history. They've never seen anything like it. You're getting a fifty share every week. You're all over the newspapers, Digby's every woman's fantasy, and you're the darling of TV *Guide*. If you want to, you can own this country."

Peter's getting a little nervous. "Soooo?"

"So, I can help you own it. I'll break my contract with the CBC and stay here. You and I will create shows together, build a production company, hire the best, and produce for the international market. It can happen, Peter, beyond our dreams. If you're willing, I won't go home. I'll stay here and we'll own Australia."

There's a quiet moment. He averts his gaze. When he speaks, it's barely above a whisper.

"Flattering," he says. "That's a great dream. And I know we could make it happen." Finally he looks up at me. "Jill doesn't like it here. We got the kids in private school—the best one. They're not comfortable here. We'll stay another year, but that's all."

By now, he's signing the bill. And I can see how sad he is. "Can I get a rain check?" he says. "Maybe another time, another country ..."

THAT'S THE LAST dinner I have with Peter, and we're both disappointed. I go back to Toronto and earn my living writing *The Tommy Ambrose Show,* a so-so series with great ideas and a less-than-fabulous star. Peter comes back the following year, joins CTV as an executive producer, supervising shows that aren't nearly as good as the one he's left.

Then, tragically, Peter MacFarlane drowns in a scuba-diving accident. He and I had a dream, and we both knew it was a good one. But we didn't see it through.

They throw a sweet little farewell party for me the night before I leave. And Digby gives me such a thoughtful present: a sterling silver boomerang with a lovely Australian topaz on it. The inscription reads, "You'll come up with something!" And sometimes I do. Maybe one day I'll come up with a way to go back to Australia. Hope so.

8

PARTNERS, PARTNERS!

*O*NE OF THE CLASSIC NEEDLE-TRADE jokes goes something like this:

Two partners are driving home from work one night when one of them says, "Sam, stop the car, we gotta go back to the office!"

"Why, what's the matter?" says the other.

"I left the safe open."

"So what're you worried about?" says his partner. "We're both here."

Good partnerships, like good marriages, are hard work. But when they work, they're worth it.

I had two good ones—one in Canada, one in the States. Both were productive for us as individuals, as well as for the team. Both partnerships made the work a lot more fun, made progress a lot faster.

If you want to be a TV writer or producer, you'd better get used to rejection—you'll get plenty of it. That's why comedy writers write in teams. You need someone to back you up, to cushion the blows. The sting from a network meeting is a lot easier to take when your partner cracks, "Those assholes—what do they know?" Hopefully, the network guys are out of earshot when he says it.

But if there's value in having a partner to help you through your lows, the highs aren't quite as high when you have to share them. You can't survive show business without an ego. But with a partner, you've got to learn to keep yours in check. And the glory, if there's glory, must be shared.

My first partnership is an arranged marriage. My maiden voyage as a variety writer on *The Jack Kane Show*—a solo trip—has been a bit rough. I love the show, but the producer is hoping for a more experienced writer and that I'm not. By mid-season, I'm running out of gas. Fresh ideas are hard to come by, and I've spent some sleepless nights trying to please a producer I find un-pleaseable. Six months of successful writing in Australia has been a confidence builder. When I get back, the CBC offers me a writing partner. To me, it's a life raft.

The writer they offer me is my old friend Stan Jacobson. Stan and I both have strong, argumentative personalities, and we fight over every line—no, every word—that goes into the script.

"That's a great idea, Rothman—a production number on an oversized Monopoly board." I thank him for the compliment. "But you've written it all wrong! It's gotta be nonstop music—can't be stop-and-go!"

"You're full of shit, Jacobson!" I say. "A ten-minute medley without comedy will put them to sleep!"

"So put the comedy in the music!" he tells me, and soon we're screaming at each other. Then we do it *his* way.

When we show up for our meeting with the producer,

we're a team again. Stan says, "Rothman has this great production segment he wrote, and I love it!"

I correct him: "*We* wrote, Stan, we wrote it together, and you're right, it's a great one!"

The producer may have been our boss, but we find if we stick together, we can outnumber him. We stick together. And by the end of the season we have the trade convinced we're the team to beat. And we are. Stan has great production ideas, I write clever musical segments. A very ordinary show becomes extraordinary. My smoke, Stan's mirrors!

STAN AND I write *The Tommy Ambrose Show* for two full seasons. Tommy is a good singer but doesn't have the personal magnetism to carry a show. So we have to come up with fresh ideas every week—big ones—to dazzle the audience with. We're never short of fresh ideas—musical segments based on comic book characters, parlor games, Broadway shows—and lots of things that play to our star's strengths. He sings well, does good impressions, so we create a segment that pays tribute to a different singer every week. Tommy scores in it. CBC gives us full credit for what we're doing, and our stock begins to rise. We're learning our craft, becoming real writers.

But make no mistake about it, our eyes are already turning southward. Whatever praise CBC is heaping on us isn't enough to counter the allure of BTASB—Big-Time American Show Business. We want it! No, not for the money, for the professionalism. Okay, we want the money, too. Mostly, we want to see our ideas produced with the kind of pizzazz the big-time American variety shows get—from great performers and sets and costumes and lighting and music. CBC can't afford those things. So we make monthly trips to New York

City—then, the capital of U.S. television—hoping to break in. We hire an American agent—Harry Steinman—a real cigar-chewing, Damon Runyon type. Harry sets up meetings with U.S. producers, assuring them that no TV show is too big for "his boys." We show them flashy film clips of our work, pitch them ideas for new shows—anything to break through. At night, Harry takes us to the Stage Delicatessen, where all the comics—big time and small time—hang out. What a thrill. Milton Berle comes over, and Harry introduces us as writing stars of tomorrow.

"How old are you kid?" Uncle Miltie asks me.

""Twenty-eight," I reply.

"Cute," he says. "I got ties older than you!"

One-liners and pastrami sandwiches—heaven! We feel good about our chances. We'll make it.

But alas, it isn't to be. Our meetings produce nothing but turn-downs. And Stan gets discouraged and frustrated, decides to pack the team in. CBC has offered him a director's job, and he's determined to take it. I'm crushed. We've worked together so hard. I try to dissuade him—success is just around the corner, I say—we'll break through. But there's no convincing Stan; he wants what he wants. Can't blame him.

Barely six weeks later, I get the break—the one Stan and I were waiting for. On a big-time American show. In fact, CBS's biggest! U.S. television is moving west, and I'm moving with it. I'm off to Hollywood. I don't know it yet, but I am about to become the youngest writer on the *Judy Garland Show* staff.

{ 9 }

WHICH SIDE

OF THE

RAINBOW?

*J*UDY GARLAND IS THE FUNNIEST woman I've ever met. Also the best raconteur and the most fun to be around. No one can hold an audience like Judy, on stage or off.

She's in her early forties when CBS gives her a TV series. I'm twenty-eight, a neophyte comedy writer, when we meet. I've just crossed the border, looking for work. Imagine! A kid writer from Canada arrives in Hollywood, and two days later he's writing for Judy Garland.

I'm not there in search of fame and fortune. I'm in the middle of a contract dispute with the CBC, which put a take-it-or-leave-it offer on the table. Arrogant little fool, me, I leave it! Three days later I'm on my way to the big time, armed with nothing but a short résumé and my dubious wits. My friend Saul Ilson invites me to stay at his house for a few days while I look around. (Three months later I move out.) Saul picks me up at the airport, tells me he's arranged a meeting the next day with *The Judy Garland Show*'s new producer, Gary Smith. Saul is sure I'll get the job, and he's right. So now you know the secret of success in show business: it's not *what* you know; it's *who* you know. And if you buy that one, I've got a toll bridge in upstate New York I can let you have for peanuts. But I digress...

Wizard of Oz made Judy Garland a star at age sixteen. She could sing, act, dance—she could do it all. She starred in movies, concerts, TV specials—what a career! But she never starred in her own life. She had to cope with a relentless stage mother, a ruthless studio boss, and a slew of husbands who would do anything for her but let her lead a normal life.

All of this is common knowledge, so the angst in her personality comes as no surprise. What surprises me is the personal warmth, kindness, charm, and humor she shows everyone—especially the little people. This is a woman who sincerely cares. And contrary to George Burns's thesis, you can't fake that.

Judy's closest friends are the ones she grew up with in MGM's stable of child stars: Mickey Rooney, June Alyson, Donald O'Connor, Freddie Bartholomew, Roddy McDowell. They're thrown together as kids, remain friends as they become stars, know each other's trials and tribulations, trust each other till their last days. Sadly, their studio boss, Louis B. Mayer, makes them compete with each other for the best roles, and what child wouldn't become neurotic, forced to compete with her friends?

Judy's MGM gang is, one by one, booked as guest stars on the TV series. Charming, they are, and talented. Maybe a little high-strung from the lives they've led. Or haven't led. They all tell stories about the Louis B. Mayer days. Funny stories, horror stories. According to Judy, Louis B. told her and June Alyson that a huge role was coming up and he couldn't decide which one of them to give it to. He kept both of them on edge, then told them the picture had been canceled. Judy makes it sound funny, but to my mind, it isn't. The man was a monster. Louis B. Mayer took a bunch of very talented kids, stole their childhood, gave them fame in its place. But stardom was no substitute for love, and Judy could never get enough love. She would talk about her tortured youth and make it all sound funny. But it wasn't funny. She had no life but the life she led on screen. There she'd get all the love she needed. For the moment. Then she'd feel empty again.

I'm still wet behind the ears when new producer Gary Smith hires me to write Judy's series. My first show in Hollywood, and my God, it's stressful! Jim Aubrey, CBS's fearsome czar, known around town as the smiling cobra, has already fired the first *Garland Show* producer and his writing team. The atmosphere becomes incredibly tense when Aubrey shows up, always flanked by a couple of his hatchet men. We all wonder who'll go next.

This is nothing like the collegial small-town climate I've grown up in. Toronto's cozy TV community is writer friendly. This is the big time. It pays more, much more, and the folks back home think I'm doing terrific. But I'm not ready to swim with sharks yet. I make up my mind that my first show in Hollywood will also be my last.

There are five shows in the can when I get there. Jim Aubrey hates them all. Gary screens them for me so I will know what *not* to write.

You're kidding, Gary. Those shows are terrific! Why on earth would they fire the staff that produced them? And how on earth can we possibly do better?

Gary explains: CBS secretly tested the first five shows with a live audience, and the results were poor. People didn't like Judy up close and personal. Too emotional, too dramatic, too exotic, too neurotic. They don't relate to her as they relate to the everyday sort of person Dinah Shore seems to be. So CBS in its infinite wisdom decides to make Dinah

Shore out of Judy Garland. Wrong! Can't be done. And we prove it with the next ten or twelve shows. But then I doubt that we could make Judy Garland out of Dinah Shore either. Judy was Judy. Dinah was Dinah. But *you* try telling a network president that he made the wrong choice giving Judy Garland her own weekly series.

JUDY ALWAYS HAS a good time working. And she keeps us laughing, too. Whatever nasty stuff is going on in the private network offices—and there's plenty—Gary keeps away from us. And to my good fortune, Norman Jewison, my former boss and friend, gets hired as the show's executive producer. Norman, and the always supportive Gary Smith, protect the new boy (that's how I'm labeled) from the slings and arrows of outrageous politics.

And there are plenty of those. The head writers I report to (they keep me out of any and all meetings with the producers) are a team of unscrupulous hacks who are forced on us by the network. They steal ideas wherever they can, take the credit, then complain that they aren't getting enough help from the writing staff. Writing with them is *not* fun, and their brand of humor is all wrong for La Garland. All schtick, none of the warm humor that Judy delivers so well. I'm constantly at odds with these men. So is everybody—the other writers, the producers, the director—but we all do our best to contribute to the fabulous woman we're working for.

One day Norman stops me in the corridor: "How come I'm not getting much of your material for the show?" Norman is genuinely disappointed. He knows I'm a capable writer.

"Norman—you used three of my pieces on last week's show. Two the week before. I've had at least one piece of material on every show." I name some of them. Good pieces.

"Oh," he says, knowingly, but says no more.

A week later Gary confides in me: the head writers want to get me fired. "How come?" he asks them, nonchalantly. "Isn't he being productive?"

"Not really," they say. "He's a good kid, but there's not much of his stuff we can use."

But Norman and Gary know differently, so there's no way they're going to let me off the show. I work hard every day, learn my lessons, and avoid politics whenever I can. It's a tough show for all of us. (Norman later says it was his toughest.) But Judy is what makes it all worthwhile. She's always gracious about the material we give her, and you can count on her giving 100 percent of herself every performance. She makes us look awfully good.

She enjoys her work—jokes a lot, laughs a lot, gives her all for every rehearsal. She also gives full support to the other performers on the show. Invariably. All except one time when she didn't. And I don't know whether it was on purpose or not.

We all go down to the Coconut Grove to see this new singer who has just burst onto the scene. Barbra Streisand. She introduces Judy in the audience, does an amazing act. So we book her on the show.

Is it fear, self-defense, or just a coincidence that Judy comes down with laryngitis the week Barbra is on the show? Judy just can't rehearse. Barbra is nervous—this is the big time, unfamiliar surroundings. Judy comes in just for dress rehearsal, can barely talk. She and Barbra mark their positions, never rehearse full out. Poor Judy has to save what little voice she has left. Barbra is very sweet with her, hovering like a mother hen. Judy seems frail; we're all very concerned. Then the audience comes in, the orchestra strikes up, and the real Judy Garland takes stage. Lights! Camera! Garland!

Streisand doesn't know what hit her. To her credit, she fights back valiantly, catches up, and the two divas sing gloriously together. Happy days are here again! Anyone who caught that performance will tell you how great those two angels sang. It was unforgettable!

Who wins the battle of the divas? It's a draw. Would it have been so without the help of laryngitis? *Quién sabe?* Superstars have to learn how to get to the top. They also have to learn how to stay there.

JUDY ALWAYS HAS a good time working, sometimes too good. She loves June Alyson, and the two of them cavort in rehearsals all week. When the audience comes in, the girls are a little tipsy from too much Liebfraumilch, slurring their words as they sing to the live audience, finish their song and dance routine by falling right off the stage into the audience's lap. Mort Lachman, Bob Hope's producer, is sitting beside me, and he whispers into my ear, "Loved their Dean Martin impression!"

SEE WHAT I mean—this really isn't a memoir. If this were a memoir (notice, I use the subjunctive to denote a contrary-to-fact clause), I'd be telling you all about my own career, making myself the hero of it all. Like Mel Torme did in his memoir, *The Other Side of the Rainbow.*

Mel, a well-established jazz singer in his own right, is a music writer and occasional performer on Judy's series. He's a big talent. Only thing bigger than his talent is his ego. I meet Mel my first day on the job:

"What do ya do, kid?" he asks, like I'm the butler or the upstairs maid.

"I write," I say, faking modesty.

"Oh, yeah? Ya write comedy sketches?"

"Uh-huh."

"Dialogue?"

"Uh-huh."

"Stand-up monologues?"

"Uh-huh." In Canada you have to write everything just to make a living. But Torme doesn't like what he's hearing. His eyes narrow. "You don't write special musical material, do ya, kid?" (He knows what I do—Gary's already told him.)

"Sure I do," I say, flushing my career down the toilet.

"Not on this show, ya don't! That's *my* specialty."

Well, la-dee-da, Mel! Musical material is my specialty, too. It's what they hired me for; it's what they're gonna get. "Nice meeting you, Mr. Torme," I say, as I leave his office. He hasn't scared me one bit!

When Mel Torme wrote his book, he made it sound like he was the only one on staff who knew anything, did anything, contributed anything. He bad-mouthed everyone, wrote himself in as the hard-bitten hero who showed up in time to save poor, defenseless Judy from all us bad guys. It just wasn't true. We had a very talented creative staff doing the show. Top-notch! With a lot less ego than Mel's. Torme's memoir was an ego trip—pure fiction.

Five years after Mel's book comes out, I get a call from an author who says he's writing a book about Judy's series. I figure it's a joke. It's not.

"Tell me about Torme," he says.

Couldn't believe my ears. "You really wanna know?" I say. Then I spew my guts out, chapter and verse, my version of the story. All about Torme's ego, how awful he'd been—ugly!

"That's real interesting," says the writer.

"Am I the first person on the staff you asked that question?"

"No, you're the ninth," he says.

"Wha'd the other guys say?"

"You were the kindest," he says, and hangs up.

I read the book when it comes out, and what the writer had said was true—we all got even with Torme. And I'm thrilled.

See, that's what happens when you write a memoir—you get bitchy!

DURING MY TERM on *The Judy Garland Show,* Wayne and Shuster come to visit. To refresh your razor-sharp memory, Johnny Wayne and Frank Shuster are Canada's reigning kings of comedy. They have more spots on *The Ed Sullivan Show* than a leopard with the measles. They began as kids on a radio series and went on to become comedy superstars of the Canadian TV network. Amazing, since Canada didn't allow superstars to develop on its TV network. Except Wayne and Shuster. And only after the boys had made it big on *Sullivan.*

Johnny leaves word that he and Frank are in town for meetings with their agent and would like to have lunch. (Notice, I didn't say "do lunch"—that would be too un-Canadian for W & S.)

So I call him back at the Beverly Hills Hotel: "Johnny Wayne, please," I tell the operator.

Ring, ring, ring. Then, a groggy voice: "Hallo..."

"Johnny, is that you?"

"Yeah, who's that?"

"Bernie. Bernie Rothman."

"Oh, hi, Bernie, how ya doin'?"

"Fine. Johnny, you okay?"

"Sure, why?"

"You don't sound like yourself."

"Just got in from the studio. Bit tired, that's all."

"Good, good. How's Frank?"

"Frank? Frank? Hey, Bernie—you sure you got the right John Wayne? You want the Duke or the comedian?"

We both laugh. "I'll call again and get the funny John Wayne next time."

"Thanks. And when you do," he adds, laughing, "tell him this John Wayne is getting sick and tired of getting the other John Wayne's phone messages!"

SO I HAVE lunch with Wayne and Shuster, and they tell me this story. A week ago, their take-no-prisoners U.S. talent agent, Marty Cummer, calls Johnny in Toronto, very excited: "We got it, Johnny, we got it!"

"Great, Marty, what've we got?"

"The comedy series. CBS gave us an offer for thirteen 'firm,' no pilot necessary. Congratulations, boys, *The Wayne and Shuster Comedy Hour* is on the air!"

Johnny takes a deep breath: "Marty—I told you—we don't want to do a series in the U.S. We'll do specials down there, but if we do a series, we'll have to move to L.A."

"What's so terrible about that? The climate's great, the living's good—lots of kosher delis—you and Frank'll love it down here!"

"But Marty, we've got families—wives, kids—we grew up in Toronto—lifelong friends. We're happy here!"

Marty gets pensive: "Yeah, well, some day you'll learn, Johnny. There's more to life than just happiness."

Okay, I give up!

Johnny tells me the story over lunch (later confirmed by Cummer as true), asks me my feelings about working in Hollywood.

"Well, in one way it's more secure than working in Canada," I say. But judging by the look on Johnny's face, he doesn't believe me. "The volume of work here is great. So if your boss is giving you a hard time, you just tell him off and move on to your next job. You do that once in Canada and your career is over."

"So you like working here better?" says Frank.

"Nope. I miss the camaraderie in Canada, the enthusiasm, the passion. I'll finish out my contract on Garland and go back."

I can't tell them the *whole* truth. At the time, the working atmosphere I'm experiencing in Hollywood is poisonous. So much tension and fear, it takes all the joy out of writing.

So Wayne and Shuster turn down the CBS series. And, after six months in the big time, I go back to Toronto. Because Johnny and I both believe there is nothing more important to life than happiness.

10

WITH MY
TAIL BETWEEN
MY LEGS

*O*KAY, MAYBE I'M NOT TOUGH
enough for the big time. Between Mel
Torme, the head writers, and the CBS hoodlums, every day
has been brutal. Writing for weekly television is a tough
enough gig—you don't need that kind of personality clash
on top of everything else.

Gary Smith calls. He wants to pick up my option—to
write Garland for the rest of the year. So damn gracious of
him. I tell him I'm burned out, ask for a rain check. Sure.
Then Norman calls. They really want you, he says. He knows
how insufferable the head writers were, but they've been
fired. I'll love the new guys. Don't give up on Hollywood—
this was just an impossible show. I thank him for his kindness, but I just don't have the strength to continue. I want to
be back home in Toronto with my family, figure out what I
want to be when I grow up. He understands.

So I wing back to Toronto. I don't feel defeated, just a
bit beaten up. Kinda like I fell off my horse. I'm tired, I'm
weary, I'm running on empty. No work in sight. Hope CBC's
forgiven me for leaving them. Rest first, worry later.

Big surprise! CBC gives me a hero's welcome. The Toronto crowd got word that Rothman spurned a U.S. contract extension to come back to Canada. (Wonder who spread *that* around?)

I get my choice of shows to write, spend a well-paid year and a half writing anything I want, 'cause I'm a local boy made good. I write my first drama—*Clown of a Thousand Years*—the story about a hard-nosed comic that traces the history of comedy as it tells the story of our anti-hero's sordid personal life. Everyone's surprised at how well it turns out. Especially me! Then, my first sitcom pilot—*The Smothers Brothers,* in a comedy-adventure spoof. It isn't great, but good enough to use as a pilot to get the Smothers their own sitcom on NBC. Next comes my first all-original musical comedy—*Blame It on Love,* a sexy story with a jazz score. It surprises no one that offers start coming in from the States. Except me—I'm surprised. And frightened. Big-time U.S. television is scary, not a lot of fun. In Canada, work seems stress free, warm and fuzzy. Safe. Still, the U.S. TV game is a challenge. I don't know what the hell to do.

Well, maybe a few U.S. specials won't hurt. First, *The Bell Telephone Hour* I write in New York for Gary Smith. He's a delight to work for, and the show goes well. And stress free. Then, a Rowan and Martin special (pre-*Laugh-In*), we shoot in San Francisco. Not a great show, but I'm the head writer, and I sure have fun in that town. So I'm starting to reconsider the U.S. possibility . . . maybe for the right offer . . .

Any horseman will tell you that the better riders ride better horses and fall off more. One sure way never to fall off is never to get on. But you won't experience the excitement of horseback riding.

So, big deal, I fell off a horse! I'm getting back on.

11

A FAMILY

OF KINGS

*W*HEN I FINALLY GET BACK ON MY horse, back to Hollywood, it's at the behest of my old friend Saul Ilson. Saul is producing his first U.S. network series. It's TV variety, built around an all-American family of singers—the King Family—everything you'd want your family to watch together. The four King Sisters, pretty-girl band singers, with husband Alvino Ray's orchestra. They're attractive middle-aged women, surrounded by their lovely daughters, sons, grandchildren—a beautiful sight on a Saturday night, with harmonious blends from the American song book.

Saul wants a writer he can trust on his first producing assignment. And I want something sturdier than the Garland series to cut my American teeth on. Maybe this time it won't hurt.

The offer is a good one: a full season, with good pay, working an easy show, headed by a trusted friend. I take it. Move my family down, rent a modest house in Beverly Hills, put the kids in school, get my green card (it was simple in those days), and go to work on Easy Street for the rest of my life. Yeah, right!

Within weeks, I find myself in the depths of depression. I have money, I have security, I have prestige, I have family, I have friends—there's nothing I don't have. It's terrible not to want anything. And that's where I am, with nothing to want. The kids are making friends in school, Saul is pleased with my work, the show is going well, and I'm wandering the streets of Beverly Hills every night, looking for something to worry about. Maybe there's something wrong. There has to be more to a Hollywood career than stringing songs together for this family of angels. Or writing cute dialogue for their grandchildren. I need new goals. All the old ones have been fulfilled, and none of that seems to matter. I'm pretty sure I want *something*. But what? Where is it? When would I find it? Would I ever do anything worthwhile with my life? Otherwise, I might just as well have stayed in Dad's business. No good! The one thing I know for sure is that I'm a creative man, and I have to do creative things. Should I write a novel? Could I? I'd have to invest a year of my time with no guarantee of reward. A musical comedy for the stage? Maybe. But I've already failed at theater. And why isn't my home life filling the void? I love my kids, but that isn't enough. There's a heaviness inside me that I'm lugging around and just can't get rid of.

I'm depressed. Deeply. I should talk to someone. Maybe Saul. Maybe my wife. Maybe a shrink. Someone. But I'm afraid to tell anyone how lonely I feel. How lost I am. I've worked my butt off getting everything I wanted, and now none of it is making me happy. How can I admit that? Doesn't that make me just another spoiled brat?

I need to shake things up a bit. I go to Saul—ask to get

off the show. He laughs. "Come on, Bernie, it's the middle of the season. You're writing great, and I need you. If I wanted to let you go, I'd fire you. That way, at least you'd collect unemployment insurance. Now what's wrong?"

"Nothing," I say. "Nothing. Guess I'm just feeling a little blue."

"A little blue?" he shouts. "A little blue? And for this you wanna quit the show? Go get laid, Bernie, or get drunk or get crazy, but for chrissake get rid of what's bothering you. 'Cause I'm not letting you off the show!"

I CAN'T FIND my way out of my funk, so I start drinking. I've never had a drinking problem, but it's an easy habit to acquire. I just don't want anyone to notice. So every night, before I schlep home from the Hollywood Palace, where we tape *The King Family*, I have a nice big mug of hot coffee. Spiked with six ounces of cognac—French cognac, the good stuff—and then ride home on my motorcycle. What was I thinking? My wife says it sounds like a guy who's trying to kill himself. Probably would have, but a couple of cops saved me.

I'm on my way home one evening, high as a kite on my motorcycle, weaving and bobbing, doing a kind of waltz to my inner music, when I notice an orange light flashing on and off in my rear-view mirror. How colorful, I'm thinking. Then the patrol car pulls me over, and two burly cops get out. One of them comes over as I get off my bike.

"Did you know you were doing thirty miles an hour back there..."

"Officer, this is a thirty-mile zone."

He finishes his sentence: "...through a stop sign?"

By now he's leaning in, smells the cognac on my breath.

"Had a drink or two?"

"One or two," I answer, smiling, holding up four fingers.

He's not smiling. He points to the other cop who's drawing a chalk line down the middle of the sidewalk. "Think you can walk that line?" he asks.

"I think I can walk all three of them."

I laugh; he doesn't. I'm not quite in control of my faculties, and he knows it.

Teeter, teeter, an enormous struggle, but I walk the line. Again I'm smiling. He's furious.

"Mister, you've gotta be crazy!" he screams. "You're lucky you're not dead!"

I come to my senses; I bow my head.

His voice softens: "Are you a man of your word?"

"Yessir, I am." Remember—you can't fake sincerity.

"Here's a ticket for going through the stop sign." I take the ticket. Then: "Mister, I know you're drunk. So here's the deal—catch ya again, you're in jail for a month. And I *will* catch ya. Got that?"

"Yes, sir, yes officer."

"Now get outta here. I just saved your life."

Probably did. But he didn't cure my depression. Bummer!

12

THE KID

FROM

BROOKLYN

*I*T'S DANNY KAYE WHO CURES ME OF my depression. Gets me back on track, excited about show business again. *The King Family* had ended and I'd made up my mind that television wasn't for me. It was too stressful, not creative enough. I had to find something that would satisfy me on a deeper level. Re-runs of *The King Family* would be playing all summer long, and I would be paid half my original fee for each one. Which meant I'd have enough money to take my family to Portugal, rent a villa on the beach for six months, get over my depression, and write the great American/Canadian novel. (Take your pick.) How's that for a plan, eh? Never happened. And if you're wondering why Bernie Rothman never wrote the great Canadian/American novel, blame it on Danny Kaye.

I was ten when I first saw Danny Kaye in a movie. *Up in Arms* was a World War II comedy that introduced Danny to the masses (before that he had been a cabaret performer). I was one of the masses.

Danny was an unlikely movie hero. He wasn't handsome, strong, or courageous like other leading men. (Consider John

Wayne or Clark Gable—not too bright, but quick fisted enough to win the damsel and the day.) Danny seemed the sensitive type—I could identify with that—kind and warm and gentle, with a sense of humor that got him the girl ("Git-gat-gittle") and a wackiness that usually outsmarted the bad guys ("The vessel with the pestle..."). He also had his brilliant wife, Sylvia Fine, writing special songs for him—musical monologues sung by eccentric characters that were tailored to Danny's unique talents ("Anatole of Paris").

I saw all of Danny's movies. Some of them a dozen times (*The Secret Life of Walter Mitty, Hans Christian Andersen*). They were delightful, and so was he. So it wasn't surprising that I ended up writing for Danny Kaye. I knew his work better than he did.

It's just a few days after we finish taping *The King Family*. My agent, Stuart Robinson, calls, very excited, to tell me he's made an appointment with the new producer of *The Danny Kaye Show*. "There's one opening left on the staff, and every writer in town wants it."

"That's great, Stu, but I'm not one of them. I still have the blues."

"I thought you liked Danny Kaye."

"I love him. It's Hollywood I don't like."

Stuart is disappointed. "Come on, Bern, give it a chance. You've only been here a couple of years, and you've done pretty well. You're making a name for yourself; we're building your career."

"Stu, I really appreciate all you've done, honest. I'm just not comfortable being a writer in this town. It's not satisfying."

"So you're going back to Canada?"

"I've been thinking about it—I'm not sure. I may go off to Portugal with my family and write a novel."

"Write a novel—great idea! But first you'll take the meeting. You owe me, Bernie. And the new producer is a terrific guy, trust me—you'll love each other."

So I do, and we do. After the meeting, Stu phones: "He loved you! We'll have an offer by the end of the day."

"Stu, I'm going to Portugal and..."

"Of course you are. You'll have a wonderful vacation and come back and write *The Danny Kaye Show*. Danny's dying to meet you."

Those are the magic words. 'Cause I'm just dying to meet Danny.

PICTURE THIS: I'M twenty-nine, riding my motorcycle up Danny Kaye's driveway with mixed emotions. On the one hand, I'd love to write for Danny Kaye—he's the greatest. On the other hand, I'm already exhausted from the nasty politics of BTHSB (Big-Time Hollywood Show Business). It's too intense, too cutthroat—too high a price for me to pay. I've got a wife and kids (three of my five have already arrived on this planet and are consuming food at an alarming rate). I want to go someplace quiet and write the great Canadian/American novel. Then I deal myself a third hand: what if I can't write the great Canadian/American novel? Or any other kind of novel? I wind up with no novel and no Danny Kaye, whom I know I can write for. I was practically weaned on his material. And if Mr. Kaye really wants me to write his show, how can I turn the man down? Maybe I'll get to Portugal later.

Danny Kaye greets me at the door. In person. I'm impressed. He leads me into the breakfast room, where Stanley Prager, his producer and my new best friend, is waiting. Yadda, yadda, yadda, we sit down for breakfast. Already

I'm disappointed, because instead of one of Danny's famous French omelets (he's a renowned chef), he produces a plate of store-bought cookies. So how bad can he want me? He passes the cookies. I take six as he pours my coffee, and I hear Stanley say: "Go ahead, Danny, ask him anything."

Danny feels a little awkward, so he takes on an acting role. "Tell me, young man—do you really *vant* to write my show?" he asks in a Viennese accent. A rhetorical question. But my answer is unrhetorical: "No... I haven't decided yet." Blunt, but they laugh. I'm trying to be honest, and they think it's a joke.

Danny follows up, again as the old Viennese professor: "Vell, tell me this, young man—do you really think you're *capable* of writing for Danny Kaye?" They're smiling at me, staring at me, and I don't know what to say. So I tell the truth, but I tell it at breakneck speed and all in one breath.

"Absolutely, I can, but I'm not sure I want to." More laughter, but I blather onward: "See there's this novel I wanna write, trust me it's really good—I'm no Dostoevsky—more like a Zane Grey—but there's a perfect beach in Portugal where you rent a villa with your own cook for two hundred dollars a month—two hundred a month! Can you imagine—you couldn't rent a broom closet here for that—which means I could stay for six months and write—well, maybe not the *great* American novel, but a pretty good one—and I'd say six months is enough time to get a fairly good novel started—after all, it took Dostoevsky eleven years to finish *War and Peace*—or was that *Crime and Punishment*—no, that took me eleven years to *read*—but honestly, I don't know if I'm capable of writing even a mediocre novel in six *years* so what do I do? I know damn well I can write for Danny Kaye—he's my favorite actor on this entire planet, and honest, Mr. Kaye, it would be a privilege for you to hire me—no, for me to hire you—no that's not it either! What the fuck, guys, let's make a deal!"

By now they're howling. Danny turns to Stanley: "You wanna hire 'im, hire 'im. He'll be terrific." They laugh and congratulate each other as I sit quietly, praying I've made the right career move. I know my agent will be happy, but will I ever get to Portugal?

Who cares? I'm finally excited about something!

AT LAST, a challenge in BTHSB. A civilized show, run in an orderly fashion, with a staff that pursues quality entertainment. This is its third season. The writing staff, which includes the illustrious talents of Paul Mazursky, Norman Barasch, Billy Barnes, and Ernie Chambers, is a pleasure to work with. They're all secure people. So I can write comedy sketches with Paul, music with Billy, or just go off and spend a week creating one of those musical monologues that our star does so well.

Danny Kaye's premiere show of the season, and I write my first song for him. It's called "The CBS Television Rhapsody." I've concocted it by setting the new CBS television schedule to the tune of Franz Liszt's "Hungarian Rhapsody No. 2." Danny sings:

> *A Monday place for Lost In Space*
> *The Beverly Hillbillies, Tuesday's ace*
> *A Wednesday spot the Munsters fill again*
> *Thursday's Island known as Gilligan...*

The audience loves it. Fits Danny like a glove. Amazes me how quickly he learns it, how confidently he performs it. Like he's been doing it all his life. The man's a genius, and he makes me look like one, too. (Magic Johnson's brilliant playmaking always made his basketball teammates look like stars.) Starstruck, I go back to his dressing room after the show.

"Danny, that was great! I mean, you really delivered!"

He chuckles at the new boy. "I usually do," he says.

Then he gets serious. "It starts on the page," he says, a tip of the hat to me. He wants more.

I am elated, inspired. I write a new song for Danny every week: musical monologues that Danny performs as one of his characters. This one he does as a Hungarian waiter:

I'm the last of the big-time gypsies
The greatest ever been
The rest of the gypsies work for tip-sies
Playing violin!

And this one, he does as a Russian junk peddler:

I'm Petrov the Thinker
I'm very, very smart
I know you won't believe it, friends
But thinking is an art!
First you must think about something to think about
Then when you've thought it, you think it
It could be a bell or a puss-in-the-well
Or a ring or a string or a trinket!

Or Danny, as William Tell, singing to his worried son (also played by Danny) as he's about to shoot the apple off the boy's head—(to Rossini's "William Tell Overture").

I'm a darn, I'm a darn, I'm a darn good shot
Even though my eyes are not so hot
In a barn on a farm or a parking lot
I'm a darn—I'm a darn good shot

And a bunch of others. They're all solo patter songs with

lots of doggerel and plenty of good character jokes in the middle. For instance, the czar of Russia confronts Petrov with a deeply philosophical problem: "How is it—whenever I drop my bread—it falls to earth butter-side down?" Petrov thinks. Then: "Is simple—you are buttering your bread on the wrong side!"

Danny enjoys doing these numbers; they all score with the audience. I'm feeling pretty good about my work. No more blues.

But as the weeks go by, I become increasingly aware that the show's new producer (Stanley Prager has already left the show) isn't too crazy about my attitude. Maybe I'm being too pushy. A bit overconfident. And in BTHSB, writers are as disposable as Pampers. Happily, Danny likes my work, and I've got Herb Bonis, our executive producer, on my side. But I'm worried.

It's the end of the first season, and Herb takes me out to our favorite Chinese restaurant for lunch. I sense something's up, but I don't know what. Between the hot-and-sour soup and the kung pao chicken, I find out.

"Not good news," Herb says. "Our beloved producer doesn't want to pick up your option for next season."

"Why not?" I ask, very upset. "What does he want that I'm not giving him?"

"It's a personality thing," Herb tells me. "He says you challenge him on everything, Bernie, like you want to take over the show. You've got to let him be the boss."

I know Herb's right. The producer's got to be boss. "Herb . . . I'm devastated. What can I do?"

Herb gets real fatherly: "Nothing. You can't do a thing. I can. So get me a list of songs you wrote for the show. I'm seeing Danny this afternoon." Then he gives me one of his serious looks. "Now finish your soup!"

Danny intervenes with the producer. He and Herb both stand up for me. Rare for anyone to stand up for anyone in Hollywood.

Over a second Chinese lunch, Herb tells me I'm staying with the show, so I'd better write my butt off. Which I do. And if you ever catch a PBS special called "The Best of Danny Kaye," you'll see some of the stuff I wrote that season. Pretty good stuff. That's what happens when you write your butt off.

Too bad I never got to the kung pao chicken.

SO NOW I'M a big-time Hollywood writer, and I settle in for the duration. My kids are in good schools (Beverly Hills has the finest), my wife is meeting new people at the PTA, and I'm starting to think that maybe my future in California will last more than an hour and a half. At the end of my first full season, surprise—I'm nominated for an Emmy Award for writing *The Danny Kaye Show*. Bliss!

Between seasons on *Danny*, it's learning time for me. My crackerjack agent, Stu Robinson, encourages me to write shows that tell a story (variety shows do *not*—they're just a series of disconnected pieces... songs, sketches, etc.—that's why they're called variety shows). "Tell stories," he says. "That's what writers do!" So he gets me my first sitcom assignment—*My Three Sons*. I'm petrified. Haven't the faintest idea of how to go about writing it.

Today sitcoms are written by a staff—six, maybe eight full-time writers. But this is in the late sixties, when each episode is written by a single writer. You're encouraged to first come up with a "delicious notion"—something that would read well in *TV Guide*. Like they go bowling, and Uncle Charley gets his finger stuck in a bowling ball, or some such nonsense. Then, you go and pitch the notion to the story editor. And if he likes it, together you work out a story outline. Then you go away and write it, scene by scene. A first draft, then they give you notes. A second draft, more notes. Then you go away and polish it.

Okay, okay—so you wanna hear all about *My Three Sons*—my first U.S. sitcom, everyone's favorite show. What was it like? How did I get to write it? Was Fred MacMurray really that nice a guy? Were they really his sons? All right, already, I'll tell you everything, I won't hold back. But I'm warning you, you'll be bored. Easiest money I ever made!

First of all, I never meet Fred MacMurray. He only works on the show three or four weeks out of a year. So, he's long gone by the time I get there. Never meet Uncle Charley either. Or Biff or Buff or Chuck or Chick, or whatever the hell the three sons are called. Writers aren't invited to the set. Aren't necessary. By the time they begin filming, every last line of dialogue has been locked into place. They shoot the whole season without MacMurray. Then Fred comes in, and they shoot all his scenes—thirty episodes' worth—back-to-back. Piece 'em all together in editing.

The series is America's favorite, but it isn't mine. Too white-bread for me. But I want to write my way out of variety television, write stories of some kind, and situation comedy seems closest to what I've been writing. So why in the world, I hear you asking, do I end up writing for *My Three Sons,* when it's probably *The Dick Van Dyke Show* I want to write? You ask—I tell: the reason I write for *My Three Sons* is *because they let me*. See, not only do *I* want to write *The Dick Van Dyke Show,* but *every writer in town wants to*. Much hipper show. Funnier. But I have no sitcom credits, so I can't get on *Van Dyke*. I do have an ace in the hole, though, that gets me the assignment on *My Three Sons*.

My agent, the one-and-only sharp-as-a-tack Stu Robinson, also represents George Tibbles, the story editor and *éminence grise* of Mr. MacMurray's little brat pack. So how hard will it be for ace agent Stu Robinson to introduce his hotshot young writer, fresh off the highly prestigious *Danny Kaye* series, to Uncle Charley's right-hand man? Not difficult at all. And nobody has to know I can't write a joke to save my ass!

I have no idea how to construct an American-style sitcom either. To tell the truth, I could never bring myself to watch a full half-hour of Fred MacMurray & Company's family epic—not without taking at least four or five pee breaks. (It *was* kinda bland, wasn't it?) But I come equipped with a "delicious notion" to my meeting with George Tibbles, and he likes it.

The notion is about a thumping noise from downstairs that's keeping the boys up all night. They've just moved into their new house, and the thumping frightens them. It's coming from the basement, intermittently, and the boys work themselves into a frenzy, thinking maybe it's the heartbeat of a man who's buried down there. (Stole the idea from Edgar Allen Poe's story "The Tell-Tale Heart." Sort of.) The climactic scene sees the entire family tiptoeing down into the cellar in their pajamas, where the glow of their candles reveals an eerie sight—a ghostlike, white-sheeted shape. Terrifying! Cautiously, they approach, pull off the sheet, and shockingly reveal—a dilapidated sump pump. Or, should I say, "thump pump"? Thump, thump! They turn it off and go back to sleep, laughing.

A simple plot, but good enough for some tense moments and then a laugh. Show ends with three sleepy guys going off to school the next day, with a tall tale for their classmates. Delicious? I dunno...

George thinks kids will like the story, and I write it decently—at least well enough for him to accept my first draft, and do whatever little rewriting it needs by himself. Guess it didn't need much, 'cause it played all over the world, and I got royalties for decades. Three dollars at a time!

THAT SEASON, I write some action dramas, too: *The Invaders,* a science-fiction drama, produced by Quinn Martin, the man who produced *The Fugitive.* Then a Western—*The Iron Horse,* produced by my friend Steve Kandel, an amazing writer/producer who could write an entire screenplay—top to bottom—in twenty-four hours. In fine prose, too.

These men taught me how to write stories—to start with a compelling situation, get the characters involved in conflict, and simply let the story unfold. Just follow the characters, let them take you to the end. And make sure there are some surprising twists and turns along the way.

Most important, I learned to write fast-paced stories, with crisp dialogue. Every Canadian writer wants to be Shakespeare. But when you cross that 49th parallel, you learn to write with brevity, crispness, punch. That's what sells.

SO HERE I am—actually enjoying myself in Hollywood. It's my second season as a Danny Kaye writer, and I decide to make it easy on myself. I've already proved I'm a big-timer by writing a new piece for Danny every week. And notwithstanding his feelings about me, the producer reluctantly admits to Danny that I'm doing a good job. In exchange, I stay out of his way. I only write what my producer asks for. It works. Now he loves everything I write. And I never contradict him in public. (Since then, I've made it a point never to argue with anybody who's wrong.)

During this time, I manage to write several more sitcom episodes and, as my work improves, actually get to enjoy it. On one of them, "Ugliest Girl in Town," Bob Kaufman, the story editor, assures me my script is the best he's gotten. Won't let them change a word. Sure bolsters my confidence.

Working with those great comedy writers on the Danny Kaye staff, I actually learn to write a halfway decent joke. In character. And how to construct a sketch, which, to my surprise, isn't that different from writing sitcom. Just shorter. You start a sketch by putting one of the characters (in our case, Danny) in a conflict situation (his boss catches him reading a copy of *Playboy* during office hours) and watch him bungle his way to a resolution. But, of course, he comes out a winner!

Now, if all this sounds kind of technical, it really isn't. After they learn the rules, comedy writers mostly follow their instincts. Experience helps, of course. But funny is funny!

BY THE END of the 1967 season, I'm beginning to feel a bit like an American. And to my surprise, I don't mind it at all. Who'da thought? I particularly enjoy calling my relatives in Montreal, on the coldest day in February, when the thermometer reads minus forty, and telling them that because of unseasonably mild weather in L.A., I'm forced to spend another day at the beach, nursing my tan. Always goes over big!

I've started to feel like I'm part of the scene. Maybe Hollywood isn't a Sodom and Gomorrah after all. In fact, I'm finding it easy to make friends in Hollywood. Rarely on a deep level, because, the nature of the business being what it is, you never know whether your new best friend will still be here next week. (Stanley Prager, Danny's terrific producer, was fired before the season started. Don't ask me why.) Still, it's a pretty friendly place. People are more down to earth than I was ever led to expect. Like:

I'm home one afternoon; the phone rings. I answer it. A woman's voice: "Is Mrs. Rothman there?"

" 'Fraid not. Can I take a message?"

"Just tell her Joanne Newman called—Nell's mother."

"Sure," I say, and hang up.

I think about what this modest woman said. She could have said, "Tell your wife Joanne Woodward called"—she was a big movie star at the time. Or she could have said, "Tell her Mrs. Paul Newman called." Her husband was, at the time, Hollywood's biggest box office attraction. But her daughter, Nell, was my daughter Tibby's friend. And that's what this call was about.

Nice, eh?

13

THERE'LL
ALWAYS BE AN
ENGLAND

*T*WO YEARS OF VOLUNTARY SERVI-
tude on the Danny Kaye staff, and that
memorable series finally comes to a well-paid end. Big wrap-
party blast. Get to bed at three in the morning. After what
seems like two and a half hours of sleep, the phone rings
with a call from my ace agent, Stu Robinson.

"Had a conversation on your behalf with Cy Burns, great
guy, produces *The Red Skelton Show*." No "hello"—nothing.

I'm barely awake. "Oh, yeah, about what?"

"He wants to take you to London. A new series.
Interested?"

I love London. Always wanted to work there. "When?"

"In two weeks. Six weeks pre-production, ten shows firm,
then we'll see."

Desperately need coffee. "Oh, God, Stu. I don't know if I
can do it. I'm..."

"Exhausted? 'Course you are. And you've earned some
time off. Take a whole week. Then go home and pack. Treat
it like a vacation. The money's good, and they'll pay to move
your whole fakakta family to England."

Stu is the world's best agent and only slightly more of a slave driver than the average Egyptian pharaoh.

"What's it about?" I ask.

"What's what about?"

"The series. The one you want me to write in a couple of weeks. It would help to know what it's about."

"Nobody knows yet. It's a co-production between CBS and Lew Grade's English network. You guys'll make up the show when you get there. Or maybe on the plane."

Swell! "Stu, I need some time to think about it."

"Sure. How long will it take you to say yes?"

"Stuart, it's eight-fifteen in the morning!"

"I know, I got a watch. How long?"

Takes thirty seconds. Who wouldn't say yes to a trip to Europe? My English wife? My three kids? Me? I don't think so!

When I finally wake up, I'm worried. No series concept, very little time to create one, don't know the producer, not one but two major networks on our backs—nothin' but pressure. Oh well, here we go again!

IF I HAD to live in a city, I'd pick London. It's hustley-bustley, old and beautiful, noisy, crowded, crazy, sophisticated, and just about everything you'd want in a real city. I live in Los Angeles and love it. But it's not a real city.

Two weeks after Stuart's phone call, I arrive in England's capital with my family, check into the apartment-hotel curiously called the White House, and go to work every day at ATV's Elstree Studios, located in a suburb forty miles outside London. The commute is no problem. We're chauffeur-driven to work every morning and chauffeur-returned every night. Class! And on the drive, we get to know each other.

The "we" in question besides me is our U.S. producer, Cy Burns, and my writing partner for the series, Howard Leeds. They're two terrific Americans. And very, very funny ones. At night, when the wives join us (Howard is the sole bachelor), we hit all the best restaurants in London and laugh all night. What a time we're having!

The days consist of meetings with our English counterparts—we discuss what we need in the way of facilities—and they fill us in on the British talent available, many of whom are unknown to us: Benny Hill, Marty Feldman, Tom Jones, Dusty Springfield, Engelbert Humperdinck, Shirley Bassey—very talented performers, who will soon become household names in the U.S.

But our first meeting with a guest star is not with a singer or comedian, it's with the illustrious Duke of Bedford, an elegant blue blood, who lives in a grand castle, just outside of London.

"How do you do, Your Dukeship," says Cy Burns, our Brooklyn-born producer.

The Duke chuckles. "People don't call me Your Dukeship, Mr. Burns."

"What do they call you?" says Cy.

"My friends call me Ian."

"Okay, then it's Ian," says Cy.

"No, that's what *my friends* call me," says the Duke.

"What should *I* call you?" asks Cy.

The Duke thinks about this: "Would you mind calling me 'Your Grace'?" he asks.

"Only if we're dancing," says Cy.

We spend hours on the phone with U.S. talent agents, booking the splashiest American stars we can find: Milton Berle, Steve Allen, George Burns—we're doing great.

So the show's coming along beautifully. Only problem is, none of us has any idea what the show is about. Doesn't seem to bother Cy Burns. Or Howard Leeds. Two veteran variety pros. But the kid writer it bothers. 'Cause I know that if the show fails, it won't be the old pros who get blamed. They have a track record. Has to be the kid's fault.

D-day is fast approaching. As a matter of fact, we have a meeting to discuss the show with the English guest stars tomorrow morning. I, for one, have no idea what we're going to discuss. Are my partners concealing stuff from me? Probably not. Why am I the only one who's terrified?

I do the only thing I know how to do to get out of show business trouble: I write. Stay up all night and write. First, a script, then I reduce it to an outline. When the meeting begins, everybody sits down around the table and finds an outline of the show I've placed in front of them. I hold my breath. Then Cy Burns, our fearless leader, picks up the outline, studies it for a moment, and begins to explain it to our guest stars. If he's surprised at finding it, he doesn't let on. As he reads it and explains each segment, he seems fully familiar with and confident of the contents. Great actor!

And that's the show that goes on the air—I swear!

It's called *Spotlight*—not a very original title. The series is just as unoriginal. No surprise—I put it all together in one long night. Each episode has three stars. The first has Noel Harrison (former singer, now a handsome lead in a CBS spy-drama series), Abbey Lane (the sexy Latin-style singer–movie star), and English comedian Benny Hill (professional naughty boy). The format is simple, all about relationships.

The three stars do an opening number—"Come to the Cabaret"—or some such upbeat number. I write special lyrics to introduce them to each other. Then they talk together, everyone jibing Benny about his singing. The other two exit as Noel does his number—a clipped British takeoff of "The Jets" from *West Side Story*—perfect for Anglo-American relations. Then Benny and Abbey do a sketch, wherein the lovely Abbey has become insanely jealous because she is sure her husband (played by the very unlovely Benny) is cheating on her with every strumpet in town. Hysterical!

Next, Abbey does her solo number—"Big Spender," an exciting piece with Abbey playing a dance hall girl bowling over a dozen gorgeous male dancers. Followed by Benny's monologue about why the bloodless Brits had to let the over-sexed Yanks go in the first place. Everyone works with everyone, and by the end of the show, not only is the audience entertained, but you've seen the three stars come together, just as England and the U.S. have.

We use the overall idea throughout the ten-episode series, and it works. Not much depth to it, but nobody seems to mind. It's good for the stars, it's good for the audience, it's good for Anglo-U.S. relations. Both networks are thrilled. Lew Grade, the English TV czar, is thrilled, because the show has class (he pronounces it "closs")—and that's what he wants most to show the Americans. The new boy gets lots of credit for creativity (far more than I deserve), and I'm relieved that we find a hook and that I won't get fired. Which is always a writer's worry. You're worried that they'll think you've got no talent and fire you. Or you worry that they'll think you've got too much talent and fire you. Either way, writing is a sentence to lifelong paranoia. And you need support from unselfish colleagues like Cy Burns and Howard Leeds to get you past it.

And by the way—they never ask me where that original outline came from!

"COME IN, COME in, my boy. Sit down—have a cigar."

The man talking to me is Sir Lew Grade, chairman of ATV, England's most successful commercial television network. He's a large, stout, bald man, smoking a cigar that looks about two feet long. A character from a James Bond movie.

"Well, Sir Lew... ," I say as I sit down opposite him in a large Victorian office chair.

"Well, Sir Bernie... ," he answers with a twinkle in his eye and that trace of cockney in his voice. Six months ago when I arrived in England, he was just plain Lew Grade. Now he's Sir Lew. He's been knighted for good work and the millions in foreign funds he's brought into the country, selling his myriad television shows abroad. A mover and a shaker—truly a large man is Sir Lew. He continues:

"I hope my people have been treating you fairly."

It is the end of the season for *Spotlight*. Not a bad series, lots of fun with Cy and Howard, but I can't wait to get home. For the first time, I've discovered I'm a North American. I'm sailing home with my family on the Cunard Line's dowager luxury liner, *Queen Elizabeth I*. Very exciting!

"Very fairly, sir," I answer. "Generously, in fact."

"Good, good. I've seen several episodes, and I like them. You've got real class, young man. And my people like you."

"That's nice to know. We've had a fine time working together."

I wait to hear what's next. He requested this meeting—an early morning one, as Sir Lew's generally are—and I'm curious as to why. I'm sure he knows I'm sailing home next week.

"Bernie, let's talk." He leans in, careful not to blow cigar smoke in my face. "I'm planning to do plenty of business with the Americans over the next few years. My staff feel you understand us—maybe because you're Canadian—and CBS likes you too. Let's do a deal."

Wow! Am I on the spot!

"Stay with us three years. With a good bit of money. We'll do big shows with big American stars and big budgets. Are you interested?"

Gulp! Why am I going to say no? And I *am* going to say no.

I had worked too hard to get to the big time, and Hollywood *was* the big time. Big shows with big stars and big budgets are already there. The Brits are just beginning to climb the ladder. Staying with them is like going backwards for me. Yes, BTHSB is a dangerous place. But so is England, where I'm a total unknown. They're just more polite with their treachery. I've already made a good beginning in Hollywood. Why would I leave?

"I'm so flattered, Sir Lew. I've loved every minute of my stay here. But my wife hasn't been well, and I've just got to get back." Two big lies. Whoppers!

I wonder if Cy and Howard got the same offers. No, they would have mentioned it. Howard wants to stay, I know that—he has an English girlfriend. But Cy—he wants to get back to the land of fancy cars and kosher delis.

"Well, Sir Bernie," Lew says, puffing cigar smoke up at the ceiling, "maybe you should think it over. You wouldn't want to make a mistake over a decision this important."

No, Sir Lew, I say to myself, I certainly wouldn't.

I wonder if I did.

IT'S TWO DAYS later, just before lunchtime. My doorbell rings. Standing, unannounced, on the doorstep of my Victorian row house in Connaught Square is CBS's West Coast chief, Perry Lafferty, trying, unsuccessfully, to appear as if he belongs there.

"Perry—what a surprise!" That's no lie.

"Just happened to be in the neighborhood, Bern." That *is*.

"Well, don't just stand there, come in," I say warmly. But he doesn't come in, he just stands there.

"What are you doing for lunch?" he asks nonchalantly.

"Why, I'm having it with you," I say, just as nonchalantly. "Didn't we say we'd do lunch in London if you were ever in the neighborhood?"

We laugh. Perry is here with a purpose, and we both know it. He's a great diplomat, and CBS often sends him on delicate missions. But we're a long way from L.A., and I'm just the junior writer on an unimportant CBS show. What does he want?

Over lunch at the Savoy Grill, I find out. The restaurant at the Savoy Hotel, all mahogany and leather, is a pretty formal place, not, I think, randomly picked by my host. I'd been there once before in the early '50s, when it was the only restaurant in town where you could get a decent meal. (Meat rationing was still on in those days.) The bill had been less than England's national debt, but only slightly.

We're at the Savoy because Perry wants to impress, to show me he thinks this is important. He tells me of his quest over dessert, drawing on his pipe as he talks.

"Bern, CBS is doing another show with Lew Grade's outfit. In fact, the plan is to do several more. It's important to us. We trust you, they trust you. We want you to create it, write, it, steer it creatively. Tell us what you want—we'll get it for you." He's refilling his pipe, not looking at me.

My haunches rest uncomfortably on the horns of a dilemma again. But I could have expected it. Why else would Perry just "drop in"?

"I won't stay in England, Perry," I say, more securely than I feel.

"I know that. You're booked to sail home on the *Queen E.*"

"Uh-huh."

"Can't say's I blame you." Sometimes the Midwesterner comes out in Perry (he hails from Nebraska). "Suppose when you get home you create the show for us," he says, "after some time off, of course."

This plan came out of a network meeting. Perry was dispatched, ordered not to come home without signing me.

"In L.A.?"

"In L.A."

"Then what?"

"Then you come back here for a few days, meet with Sir Lew's people, agree on the format, then come and tell me what the show is."

"That's it?"

"One more thing. Once a week, you have lunch with whoever our U.S. guest star is. You're good with stars. Fill them in, tell them what you want them to do, make them feel comfortable. That's it, that's all there is to it."

I think for a moment. Then, "Perry—if I do all that for CBS, what does CBS do for me?" What a shot. I can't believe I've said it. I'm shocked. Perry isn't. He casually knocks the ashes out of his pipe into the ashtray.

"If you do all that for us, CBS will be very grateful," he says. Then he looks me straight in the eye: "Get your agent to call me, and you'll find out just how grateful CBS can be."

It ends up being a real easy job, for which I get paid enough to buy my five-bedroom house in Beverly Hills. Was I overpaid? Uh-huh. So now you know—when networks want you, not even the sky is the limit. There is no limit! That's why, like the Mounties, the networks always get their man.

The new show I create? Called *Showtime*, it's another standard variety series, set in an elegant nightclub with an audience sitting at tables around a circular frosted-glass stage with bright lights shining from underneath. That's where the guest stars perform. There's a glitzy curtain at the back of the stage through which each act enters in a multicolored floodlight. There's dancing showgirls, a bandstand with a band and a leader, and, oh yes, an American host, a different one every week, who welcomes the audience, introduces the acts, says good night, and pays for my lunch when we dine in L.A., 'cause that's what CBS wants. I meet some swell people over fine lunches in fancy restaurants in Beverly Hills: Steve Allen, Godfrey Cambridge, Phyllis Diller, Terry-Thomas, George Burns. Mostly, it's fun for me 'cause I love talking and I don't have to leave home.

CBS is happy with the show, so who am I to be picky?

14

A PRODUCER

AT LAST

*I*T ISN'T PERRY LAFFERTY WHO comes after me for a third CBS co-venture with Lew Grade's organization. It's Red Skelton's brilliant lawyer, Marvin Sears, who makes the pass. Marvin put the deals together for the first two London-based CBS shows—we know each other, like each other, and we've often talked about doing more stuff together. The stuff Marvin wants me for now is a CBS Liberace series, to fit into the Red Skelton summer slot and to continue on in the fall if the ratings merit it. The series will be shot in England. Oh, dear!

I was never a Liberace fan. The flamboyant pianist never impressed me, although I know that older audiences love him, and even I have to admit the man has a flair for showmanship. But not my cup of tea. And I've had enough of England!

"Not my cup of tea, Marvin," I tell him over breakfast at the Polo Lounge. We're sharing one of their big, gooey apple pancakes, which always make me happy.

The Polo Lounge at the Beverly Hills Hotel is a beautiful dining room, with large, green comfortable banquettes, a big bay window that overlooks a beautiful garden with a magnificent fig tree. Everyone who's anyone gathers there for breakfast. A producer doesn't need an office in Hollywood as long as he gets the right table at the Polo Lounge for his morning meeting. And the lovely hostess, Bernice, makes absolutely certain I'm well placed next to the biggies whenever I choose to breakfast there.

"I know you've got a shot with Liberace, Marvin, but I'm not your man to write it. Besides, I'd like to stay home for a while—enjoy the California sunshine. I'm a bit travel-weary." I really mean it.

Marvin never gives up. He's a charming man and the world's most persistent negotiator. He'll always find a way to wear you down.

"What would it take to get you back to England?" he asks.

"I haven't thought about it," I say.

"How about if we ask you to produce the series?" he drops in, innocently enough.

Me, shocked: "Would you?"

"If you were willing to write and create the show, too."

That makes me happier than the apple pancake. "Will you give me half an hour to pack?"

And that's how it happens. My first command of a television series—*The Liberace Show*. I want to call it *Liberace's Summer Camp*, but that's a bit flaky for the powers-that-be. Apart from that, it's a fun series to create and exciting as hell for my first producing job.

I'm amazed at how un-nervous I am. I take a couple of meetings with the star, have no hesitation about telling him what I want the series to be. He's shocked at first but then likes my ideas. Invites me to check out his vast assortment of clothes to tell him which of the colorful beaded outfits I want him to bring. (He can't bring his whole wardrobe—it would take a large battleship to transport overseas.)

Overall, I think I did okay for a first shot. I work well with the writers (although Liberace is always complaining there's too much comedy). It's a good-looking, entertaining show. We have fun with guest stars like Jack Benny, Phyllis Diller, Eve Arden, Terry-Thomas—lots of funny people. And Liberace is funny, too. Especially when he plays the piano. But sometimes on purpose. The "home-base" set is a very elegant salon, with silk wallpaper at $120 a yard. Centerpiece is Liberace's fancy white piano. I find him a snooty English butler (Richard Wattis) as a sidekick, who scowls at every new outfit Liberace wears. And a saucy French maid who keeps trying, unsuccessfully, to turn him on. (Can't remember her name, just that she was saucy.) We concentrate on comedy—lots of smart jibes about Liberace's clothes—and his piano playing, because I never take it seriously. (Not sure he likes that!)

One of the guest stars I booked on the show was Jack Benny, absolutely my favorite comedian of all time. I was overcome with joy! My brother and I had listened to him every Sunday night on the radio. The man was hilarious— built a fifty-year comedy career based on the idea that he was stingy and vain. We all knew he was neither. He was warm and generous—a teddy bear.

It's our first day of rehearsal at the Elstree Studios. "Where you staying in London?" I ask him after a few flattering remarks.

He hesitates. Then, "Oh, I'm staying at this place that overlooks the Dorchester Hotel."

I'm puzzled. I know the Dorchester, of course, but . . .

Jack explains: "I thought it would be better than paying the Dorchester's prices, overlooking this *dump* that *I'm* staying in!" His writers must have seen my question coming and armed him to the teeth.

I ask him if there's anything special he'd like to do on the show.

"Well," he says hesitantly, "I'd love to play a duet with Liberace. I play violin, you know." Like, who doesn't?

"Love to," says Liberace, when he hears. "What would you like us to play, Jack?"

"Oh, anything," says Jack. "I can play anything at all. Maybe a classical piece—I love the classics."

"Okay," says Liberace, thinking about a suitable duet. "How about 'Capriccio Español' by Rimsky-Korsakov?"

Jack turns white. "Oh, I don't know," he whines, "that's been done to death!" Sure, Jack.

We rehearse all day for a show we're about to do in front of a live English audience. I know they'll give Jack an enthusiastic response. So I introduce him saying, "Ladies and gentlemen, it's my pleasure to introduce a very brilliant man, America's greatest comedian—Jack Benny!"

Jack comes on to a standing ovation. But he has a strange look on his face as he stands beside me, taking his applause. He seems somewhat embarrassed. The applause dies down, and he says: "Bernie—that's a very nice introduction, and I thank you all for this wonderful response. But, you know, people will think I'm conceited—I mean, calling me *the world's greatest comedian*."

I correct him: "Jack—I said *America's*."

Jack scowls. "Oh," he deadpans.

JACK LOVED TO play the violin. And contrary to what people thought, he was a very accomplished musician. He enjoyed playing classical music and frequently performed to raise money for many of the world's great symphony orchestras.

I remember taking my children to meet the famous man. Jack is very gracious and charming, but he firmly lectures my daughter Tibby. "You've got to practice that cello of yours, and practice hard. One day you'll be a fine musician," he tells her. "I didn't practice when I should have, so I was never good enough—I'd give up everything if I could have had a career as a violinist."

Tibby gave up the cello shortly after that lecture. But I'll bet Jack practiced his violin till the day he died.

JACK ALWAYS WORKED clean. Never saw him work dirty—not a single dirty word. Not even suggestive. Ask anyone, they'd tell you—Jack Benny worked clean. Except once.

It's a Friars Club Roast. Roasts are traditionally dirty. This one is for George Burns, and every comic in town is on the bill. They roast George up and down for two hours. They cover everything rotten about him, including the most lurid details of his sex life. I'm told it was an uproarious evening. Finally, it's Jack's turn. As George's best friend, he's been saved for last. There's an edge of anxious anticipation as Jack gets up to speak. He looks very serious.

"You know, it's difficult to know what to say. You all seem to know George so well, and you've covered his character traits so thoroughly. But there is one thing I know about George that no one seems to have mentioned. George is a very sore loser—I mean, he gets furious when he loses." Audience begins to titter.

"Like the other night, we were playing a foursome of bridge, and George's partner was playing the hand very badly. Now I can understand him getting mad—but, I mean, calling Audrey Hepburn a cocksucker!"

I'm told the place went nuts—absolutely crazy with prolonged laughter. Jack just stands there, arms crossed, with that deadpan stare of his—and as the laughter dies down, he adds: "She denied it, of course!"

The Friars Club never recovered.

JACK DIED IN his mid-seventies, and Hollywood went into deep mourning. So did the rest of the world. My friend Herb Baker wrote the eulogy that Bob Hope delivered. Herb wasn't so much a joke writer as a very perceptive man. He ended the eulogy this way: "America knew Jack Benny and loved him. But Jack was stingy, right to the end. He only gave us seventy-six years." And for once, nobody laughed.

IT TURNS OUT that everyone loves *The Liberace Show*. It gets very good reviews and better-than-decent ratings, although not good enough to bring the show back in the fall.

Not a bad start—I give myself a B+. But how wonderful, how glorious! I finally get to be a producer, my heart's desire! Eleven years of struggle, swallowing my pride so I won't give up. Well, I finally made it. I'm a producer.

I'm about to get what I've always wanted, yearned for, longed for. And now, I'm never turning back. Never, never, never!

Well, hardly ever . . .

★ ★ ★

MAYBE IT'S TIME we talk job specs. What's the difference between a producer and a director? What do writers write besides the words? Is producing in TV the same as producing in film? How come we know the names of some successful film directors (Steven Spielberg, Martin Scorcese), but we don't know who produced their films? Or who wrote them? All good questions; glad you asked.

Film is a director-driven medium. Easy to understand why. Think back to when films were silent. They didn't need writers. The studio guys would get together with a cameraman, give him some cockamamie scenario, and he'd go out with a bunch of would-be actors and shoot some film. They'd put it together, sort of, then bring in a writer who wrote subtitles. Not exactly brain surgery. Which made the writer about as indispensable as a Bic razor.

So writers have always been the Rodney Dangerfield of cinema art—the bastard child. No one wants to admit there was a script. Not the actors, not the directors—no one. And the tradition of giving the poor scribe less respect than he deserved continued right through the beginning of talkies to this very day. The guys who perpetuated the tradition were the guys who went out there with a camera and a bunch of would-be actors (who never spoke lines) and improvised around a simple scenario. But because they ran the cameras, they were the boss over everyone. Especially the nonactor actors, who really needed someone to tell them how to act. And that, ladies and gentlemen, is how directors were born.

Television developed differently. It was a voracious medium, focusing on weekly, sometimes daily, series. No time to improvise; networks needed scripts. Fast. And actors who were skilled enough to deliver excellence in one or two takes. So good writers were much in demand and became powerful. Because they wrote not only the words that actors speak but also the action sequences, which often include a frame-by-frame description of who punches whom, where and when, and what outfit Edith is wearing when Sammy Davis Jr. comes over to visit Archie. Writers are the largest part of the creative process, and that includes everything. That's why you know the names of Norman Lear (*All in the Family*) and Steven Bochco (*NYPD Blue*) and Dick Wolf (*Law and Order*). They're great writers who create series and build creative teams that can feed the beast. And they've become the boss over everyone—including the directors, who are still telling the actors and the cameramen what to do, but now it's under the careful supervision of the writer/producer, 'cause he knows what he wants and he's the boss.

And what about that strange functionary, the producer? If I named four of my all-time favorite movies, you would doubtless recognize the names of the three outstanding directors who did them. Try. There was *Lawrence of Arabia* and *Bridge on the River Kwai*—both directed by the great David Lean. There was *The African Queen*, directed by the illustrious John Huston. And there was *On the Waterfront*, directed by Broadway's whiz kid Elia Kazan. Now, if I told you all four of these epic flicks were produced by one man, would you recognize his name? I hope you do, but I doubt you will. It was the late Sam Spiegel (originally, his screen credit was S.P. Eagle), who found all four of these properties and brought them to life on the screen. An amazing producer was Mr. Spiegel. But unlike his director contemporary, Cecil B. DeMille, Sam Spiegel is practically unknown.

The producer's function began hundreds of years ago. He was the man who raised the money, commissioned the playwright, rented the theater (sometimes he owned it), hired the actors, had the sets and costumes made, and, in the end, made a profit. Sometimes.

The producer's job is the same today as it was in Shakespeare's time. A few years back, my producing partner and I read a book called *Son-Rise*. We like it, think it would make a good TV film, so we spend a couple grand optioning the rights for a year. We then go to all three networks, one at a time, to make a "money deal." It's the third network that sees what we see in *Son-Rise* and gives us script money. We hire the writer, supervise the first draft. Not good enough. Hire a second writer. Network approves this script. Greenlight the production and finance it. So far, my partner and I haven't seen a nickel on the project. We work out a budget (can't afford to spend more than the network gives us), hire a director (a very good one), go into a six-week period for casting (including two big stars the network's gotta approve), and whaddya know, we're in production. Six months later, we've been through rehearsals, a month of filming, two months editing and sweetening (sound effects, etc.), and we deliver the movie. It gets a huge rating and great reviews. Which entitles us to start all over again from scratch on the next project. But there's a little dough left over, so our families eat this month.

Not all producers are freelancers. Many are simply hired by a studio to produce a specific project. I prefer to work on my own projects. Which means I have to find the property; option it, write it, or have it written; raise the money; hire the best possible production staff, including the director; supervise the casting; show up for every single day of production; make whatever creative contribution the project needs; keep my eye on the money; and stick with my baby like flypaper till the last frame of film has been edited, scored, sweetened, and shipped off. It's the most exciting, satisfying job of all. Believe me—I've been doing it for years!

15

BETWIXT

AND

BETWEEN

*a*FTER *THE LIBERACE SHOW,* I PULL MY writing services off the market. I'm a producer now. The big agencies all want me to sign with them, make big promises if I will. I want out of my contract with Stu Robinson, and reluctantly, angrily, he gives me my release. In retrospect, he was right, I was wrong—big tactical mistake.

I concentrate on creating new shows, which I try to sell. No luck. The agents at William Morris have been after me for years, persuade me to sign with them. It makes sense— they have the stars that will sell my packages. They are great agents—George Shapiro, Howard West. (They certainly haven't done Jerry Seinfeld any harm!) But nothing happens. Nobody's fault, but no sale. Pretty soon I run out of money. My income plummets from sixty thousand a year to twelve. I need more than that to support a family of seven. I've had two very bad years. Will I ever get another well-paying job?

During those years, I produce a couple of shows—neither pays very well, but I am happy just to work.

First, a Wayne Newton pilot, then, a couple of Bobby Gentry specials. Wayne is a great Vegas performer, but his act doesn't translate to TV.

Gentry was the sultry southern singer who wrote and recorded "The Ballad of Billy Joe," probably the biggest-selling single of the late 1960s. I can't say I wasn't overwhelmed by Bobby. She was a very seductive lady, enormously talented—a pleasure to work with. She did everything a producer could ask for. But when the show was finished, Bobby disappeared. She ran off and married Bill Harrah, the richest man in the state of California. I knew it wouldn't last, and it didn't. Neither did she. Makes me sad—she had such promise. A great songwriter, a fine balladeer. But a couple of bad marriages and some lackluster singles later and the downhill slide was complete. Bobby Gentry disappeared from show business. And so did I!

Producer jobs are murderously difficult to come by. On a variety series, there could be as many as a dozen writers, but only one producer. The producer is the boss. And everyone wants to be the boss. I wait for two years, turn down a couple of hundred thousand dollars worth of writing jobs. Stupid! Because the offers stop coming in I am losing confidence—not just in my abilities to write and produce but in my ability to support my wife and five kids (yes, there are five, now) in a comfortable way. It is frustrating. I spend all day developing projects that I've given up hope of selling. Then, go home at night to watch my wife under tremendous pressure, wondering if things will ever get better. I help her best I can, but I'm tired—battle weary. I dread the thought, but another few months of this and I'll have to sell the house. I'm lost!

So I go home. Not to my home, to my dad's home in Montreal. My folks are now divorced, and my father has remarried. I've never done this before and it feels like a defeat. My father, sensing my pitiable state, is softer and kinder than usual. I'm crying moments after I walk through his door. He's never seen me like this.

"It's all gone, Dad—my career, my confidence—and I don't know how much longer my marriage will last."

"It didn't have to be this way, my son," he says softly. "You didn't have to leave Montreal—you could be rich by now, happily married in your own home here. With all your friends and family. That's what makes me sad." He is crying by now.

"Dad, I'm having a hard time—but I made the right decision, just like you did when you left Poland. You must have had hard times, too." He nods through his tears. "I'll find my way clear just the way you did. You don't have to worry about me—I've got your blood in my veins. I'm tough, too!" We break down sobbing, hold each other real close.

Next day, he takes me out shopping, something he used to do with my sister whenever she was blue. This is a first for me. Takes me to a swank downtown men's shop and buys me half a dozen beautiful things—a suede jacket, couple of nice shirts, a cashmere sweater. I wouldn't have guessed it, but it works magic on my mood. I fly back to L.A. next day feeling a lot lighter than when I arrived.

BEING WITH MY dad always made me more practical. So when Greg Garrison, Dean Martin's hotshot producer/director, offers me a writing job, I take it. What a relief! Greg has been after me for years. I don't want to go back to writing. So what? I have to, so I do. And writing for Dean Martin is like a vacation for me. It pays a weekly salary, and I don't have to worry about producerly things like going overbudget or fighting with the network or booking stars. Just write.

I MEET JACK WOHL on my first day writing *The Dean Martin Show*. He's an advertising man, just moved out from New York, and a New Yorker all the way. He looks like one, walks like one, talks like one—never stops selling.

Comedy writing was always difficult for me. But Jack and I write easily together, and my comedy gets better. I was never very good at jokes, but my jokes improve, too. We laugh all day long in that tiny office. There are five or six little offices in the reconfigured motel in Burbank. Each houses a comedy writing team. Jack and I are the new boys, the only ones without partners, so we become partners, and for the first time in a long time, I enjoy writing.

A good partner makes you better. (That's why comedy writers write in twos.) The whole writing staff on *Dean Martin* made you better. Loosey-goosey, just like Dean, who manages to visit the show one whole day a week. Greg has ingeniously set it up that way. But his writers are quick to quip, practice on each other with fast and funny insults. One of the writers, noticing my partner's red-, white-, and blue-striped shirt, says: "Jack—you look like a man who's been buried at sea!"

Another, talking about how much he hates his former boss, says: "Whenever anyone in the world does anything rotten, this guy gets a royalty!" Easier to be funny in funny company.

Jack and I write some funny sketches—I remember one with Dean and Dom DeLuise in a restaurant, ordering rump roast while Dean's staring at a sexy waitress's luscious behind. And another, doing pansy jokes in a flower shop with Paul Lynde. Broad comedy, easy to write. Like vaudeville.

Our boss is head writer Harry Crane. Not a great writer, famous for his political skills. He can turn on a dime. Like the time he runs into our boss, Dean Martin's producer, Greg Garrison, outside a Vegas showroom, where he's just seen singer Nancy Ames perform.

"Harry," says Greg, "I didn't know you were up here. How was Nancy?"

"Terrible!" says Harry. "She can't sing, she can't dance, she can't tell a joke—no personality—nothing!"

"Sorry to hear that," says Greg. "Dean loves her—I just booked her on the show."

"Wait a minute," says Harry, "ya didn't let me finish..."

THREE MONTHS INTO the Dean Martin assignment, my agents at the William Morris office come through. Finally, I'll get my producing career back on track. Happily, it isn't a series I'm about to produce, it's a special—for Diana Ross—something I could focus on for several months; make it really good, really special! That's how I see my future in television—producing shows that are really special. Tough jobs to get, but I know I'll do them well.

I feel bad about leaving Jack, although I know we'll hook up again. And there are some terrific writers on the Martin show I know I'll miss. Most of all, it seems strange that I'm leaving *The Dean Martin Show* without ever having met Dean Martin.

Oh, well!

16

THE

PRINCESS OF

MOTOWN

*D*IANA ROSS IS ALREADY A STAR when I produce her first network special in 1971. Correction. Her first *solo* special. She has already done two NBC shows as lead singer with the Supremes, a top recording group with Motown Records. Berry Gordy, Motown's boss, is Diana's mentor and no doubt helped her with the decision to go solo. She gets real hot, real fast! Why they hire me, I'll never know. Could have had any producer in the world. I'm new and unproved—just a comer. Guess you get lucky sometimes.

So they fly me to Vegas with Berry's "right hand," the young, smart, beautiful Suzanne de Passe. Diana's act is super. Her singing features a newly released single—"Ain't No Mountain High Enough" (forgive the grammar!), and it's sensational. Perfect for her dramatic style—spoken, as well as sung—it's more like a love poem than a song. No one in the world has Diana's style—the sound of a woman desperate for love. You want to take her in your arms and love her to death. And when she moves to the music, her stunning

Bob Mackie gown moves with her. Like a dance partner—Fred and Ginger. Bob Mackie tells me she has a perfect figure for clothes—model-thin, but perfectly shaped.

On a lighter side, she sings, "Reach Out and Touch"—warm and waltzy. By the third verse, she has the entire audience holding hands and singing along with her. Her dialogue has the same intimate quality—cute and kittenish at times—bubbling over with humor at other times. When she does make a small slip, she laughs out loud, self-mocking—and you love her for it!

Flying back with my coproducer, Jerry McPhie, we congratulate each other on our good fortune—we're in charge of a show that will be a big hit.

Not so fast! Berry Gordy has built Motown into a vast music empire without our help. He isn't about to give up control of one of his crown jewels just because he's new to television. He is a rags-to-riches success story—just like my father—and like my father, he can never be wrong, never back off. He owns the package, and we'll have to prove ourselves every inch of the way.

Jerry and I hire the staff, get our own suite of offices, ten minutes from Motown central. I start working with the writers on day one, sketching a format, listing guest stars, everything producers do to put the show together. Unbeknownst to us, Suzanne and her staff are doing the same thing behind us. The battle lines are drawn at that first meeting.

Suzanne kicks it off by saying: " 'Ain't No Mountain High Enough' is gonna be a monster hit. So we're opening the show with Diana singing the song high up on top of a mountain." Her minions are impressed.

Being young and stupid, I say: "No, we're not doing that."

Suzanne is surprised. "Why not?"

"I can't exactly pinpoint why I don't want Diana to sing 'Ain't No Mountain High Enough' on top of a mountain, but I'd have the same reaction to her singing 'Time On My Hands' on a clock." Talk about arrogance!

World War III breaks out, us against them. They want to reflect the times—a much more aggressive show, asserting Diana's roots. We see Diana as a crossover artist, who should play to a wider audience. "White folk" will be offended by a militant "black" stance. It's the early '70s—Watts isn't that far behind us, and people are touchy. In the end, Berry sides with us. And I apologize to Suzanne for being arrogant. Not that I've ever really been arrogant...

FIRST MEETING WITH Diana is in Berry's office. We are at a standoff about choosing guest stars. Suzanne and her gang are determined to try for big movie stars who have never guested on a TV show. Pretty naive. We point out that if they've never done it before, they are unlikely to do it now. Diana hopes to land the "red hot" Paul McCartney by putting their personal relationship on the line. I thinks it's a bad idea. But she calls him at home, and we listen on the speaker phone.

"Paul..."

"Yes, Diana. How are you?"

So far, warm. We're heartened.

"Paul, I'm very excited. They've given me my own TV special."

"Oh, Diana, that's great. Good luck with it."

So nice, that Liverpool charm!

"Paul, I want you to be my very special guest star. We could sing together, talk, have some fun. Will you do it?"

Still warm: " 'Fraid not."

Devastated: "Oh, Paul...why not?"

A beat. Then, thoughtfully: "Because I don't want to."

I don't remember the rest of the conversation, though I'm sure it was cordial. He had hurt her feelings. Hadn't meant to, but as Berry later remarked, "the man is *painfully honest*." No matter how close Diana's friendship with Paul, our guest stars would be Bill Cosby, Danny Thomas, and the Jackson Five—not a bad lineup. And Motown learns the facts of life about booking guests on TV—stars invariably do what's right for their own careers. Friendship comes second.

THE MEETING IS at Diana's house—Jerry and I and Suzanne—to introduce Diana to our choreographer, Jaime Rodgers. I've worked with Jaime before—very bright, very versatile, and tough enough to stand up to the whims of any star. He began his career as a dancer in the original cast of *West Side Story*—an enormously creative man.

The main thrust of the evening is to discuss what we feel will be a centerpiece for the show: a silent-movie sequence featuring Diana as Charlie Chaplin, Harpo Marx, and W.C. Fields. A very demanding piece of pantomime. Ms. Ross needs no help from us with her singing. But a piece like this showing off her ability to characterize will establish her bona fides as being more than just a pop diva. It's new to Diana, and we worry—will she pick up the challenge?

Are you kidding? She loves it! Trouble is, she has no idea who Harpo Marx and W.C. Fields were. What's that? You're not surprised? Mean to tell me that no one younger than my grandfather is familiar with those silent-movie icons? Okay, so I won't ask *you* to do *your* impression of a Chaplin walk, a Harpo grin, or a W.C. Fields scowl. But such is our scenario that Diana will have to perform all three. And such is her talent that after viewing some films of each of these masters, she and Jaime create a tour-de-force out of our modest scenario. We set it all to player-piano music, and what results is an elegant, comedic "silent-film suite" that has the critics raving. And I'll bet anyone who compares Diana's fine impressions with the filmed originals will declare Diana the winner. Or at least, make it a draw. She is brilliant! And then some!

Diana is brilliant right through the show. Not just her singing, which is always brilliant. She is brilliant with Bill Cosby playing his little girlfriend, Fat Alberta. (Can you believe it? Bob Mackie's dress actually makes Diana look obese.) She is brilliant with Danny Thomas, screwing him up as he attempts to teach her the art of joke telling. And she is at her brilliant-est as she pantomimes the silent-movie legends. What a talent!

I OBSERVE TWO special relationships that make me feel good. Berry and Diana, for one, are amazing together. He discovered her, a young singer in Detroit, helped her develop into a major star. There is total trust between them—and love and respect. They call each other "blood" (meaning blood brother, blood sister). He is there for her from the beginning of rehearsal right through the taping of the show, all the while running a vast empire. I'm told he's done that through every stage of her career—always encouraging Diana, critiquing her, supporting her, laughing with her—they move together, smooth as silk. Are they lovers? Maybe—I don't know; I don't care. They are better than lovers, they are bonded—two strong, colorful personalities morphed into one. Beautiful.

The other relationship I warm to is Diana's with the young Michael Jackson. Diana discovered the Jackson Five—Michael and his four brothers—when they were just pups.

She brought them to Berry, who promptly made recording stars out of them.

Diana adores young Michael, who is maybe twelve or thirteen years old and cute as a bunny rabbit, already an accomplished, versatile entertainer. She mothers him, coaches him, applauds him. We write a comedy scene for them, with Michael playing a Sinatra-type heel, giving the brush-off to one of his "broads," played by La Diana. Hilarious! Michael is a wonderful kid to work with—lots of fun, theatrically inspired, 100 percent professional. Kinda sad, what he went through later on. I hope his hard times are past him.

17

AD — AFTER

DIANA

*7*HE DIANA ROSS SPECIAL DOES my career a lot of good. Even before it goes on the air, the boys at the Morris Agency are talking about me.

I remember meeting with Jerry Weintraub over a fancy dinner. Jerry is John Denver's famous manager. Denver's star is rising fast, and already Weintraub is negotiating network deals for him.

"I'd like to be your manager," Jerry says to me, straight out, warming his brandy snifter.

Brazenly, I ask why. "I'm a nobody producer, Jerry. Just getting started. You're a hotshot manager. You could be managing big-time producers like Ilson and Chambers. Those guys are a hit!"

"You're right, they are," he tells me, sipping his cognac. "But there's a rumor going round about you. And it's easier for me to sell a rumor than a hit."

Smart man, Jerry Weintraub. Shoulda listened to him.

JACK WOHL CALLS. He's having his troubles. Greg let him off long enough to be my head writer on *Diana*, and he did a great job. But he's impatient writing *Dean Martin*, so he leaves the show. Now we're both broke and out of work. Then we get lucky.

A couple of fast-talking salesmen, David Winters and Burt Rosen, sell Westinghouse the idea of doing a series with variety-show performer George Kirby. A thirty-minute weekly show, and we come up with the title *Half the George Kirby Comedy Hour*. Why not?

George is very versatile—he sings, he dances, he does stand-up, he does impressions, he does drugs, he does jail time. But not before I get hired to produce and head-write his series. And I bring Jack Wohl on board, split the money with him, and we spend two seasons producing the show in Canada. Jack and I learn teamwork, have a lot of fun. 'Tisn't exactly fine art, but there isn't much of that around anyway. So we'll just have to wait our turn for the artsy ones.

I LEARN A lot about producing on the George Kirby series. For one thing, I learn a producer has to be tough. George could be very combative, and I have to draw lines. Sometimes I sense he's been drinking. Very truculent! On one occasion, George doesn't do what I ask him to, and when I insist, he walks off the stage.

I call over his manager: "Charlie—George went back to his dressing room. I need him out here. Now!"

Charlie goes back, and moments later George reappears, all calmed down.

"What did he say, Charlie?"

"Well, George said you boss him around too much. You treat him like a puppet."

"And what did you tell him, Charlie?"

"I told him, 'That's right, George, you're a puppet. Now go out there and let the man pull your strings.'"

Two good men, George and Charlie. But a few years later, sadly, George goes to jail for drug trafficking.

THE SERIES IS cute—entertaining, if not memorable. There are a couple of beginnings that make me happy over the years.

The writing team of Aubrey Tadman and Garry Ferrier shows me how important writers can be. How funny, how versatile, how resourceful. And how comforting it can be, having a good writing team to support and execute your ideas. We are short staffed, so we keep them writing fourteen hours a day—send them in club sandwiches and coffee so they won't leave their room for lunch. Good sports, great writers.

Sandra Faire is my associate producer—smart and pretty and supercreative. And strong enough to scare the hell out of the wimpish execs that are her bosses at the TV station. Doesn't scare me. I know what a great producer she'll become. And she does.

And finally, I become best friends with editing rooms. I spend hours, days, weeks, months in those little dark rooms. I learn to enter them with no preconceptions. What is written and what is shot are two different shows. Maybe your opening will be a better closing. Change your sequence and you'll change your emphasis, and maybe your entire meaning. You need highly creative people in the editing room—it's going to be your last rewrite. And make sure they're people you like. Like Sandra Faire and editors Ed Brennan and John Christie. You may just be in that little dark room forever.

I RUN INTO George Kirby soon after he's been released from his two-year prison term. Sadly, I hear his combative nature had got him badly beaten up there. We hug, George and I, hearts full of emotion.

"George," I say, "I'm real sorry—sorry you had to go through it."

His eyes become watery: "I learned so much, baby—so much..."

18

THE

DOG DAYS OF

DIVORCE

*C*HANGING MY CAREER FROM WRIT-ing to producing is difficult. The jobs are scarce—everyone wants to produce (easy to fake), nobody wants to write (unfakeable). I'm feeling pretty insecure about my prospects, need help, but put off seeing a shrink. What if I learn things about myself I hate and can't change? But I'm becoming more and more troubled. My life just isn't working. Finally, I go to a psychiatrist.

I sit down opposite this elderly gentleman in his modest (by Beverly Hills standards) office and freeze up. I don't know what to say. Finally, he breaks the ice.

"Why don't you start by telling me what you'd like to accomplish here, Bernie." Reasonable question. Deserves a reasonable answer.

"Doctor—I've developed certain patterns detrimental to my career. I'm hoping you can help me break them down."

He raises his eyebrows. Is he impressed?

"Tell me about them," he says. I tell him. For half an hour I tell him how I've been shooting myself in the foot. Then he asks me a key question:

"What about your personal life, your home life—do you have a family?"

"Oh, sure, I have a great wife and five great kids. I think that part of my life is fine, Doctor. So let's concentrate on my business life—that needs work." Talk about denial!

We agree, set the next appointment, and I leave.

Three months later, I leave again. This time, it's my wife I leave. No, it isn't the psychiatrist's fault. I've come to realize I'm not getting what I need at home. The kids are wonderful, but the marriage isn't. There's nothing personal about my marriage anymore. It's all about making a living and taking care of kids. The closeness in the relationship has disappeared, and I feel I have nothing warm to come home to. I leave home.

My wife takes the children and goes to England, where her mother lives. Can't blame her. Can't blame me, either, although at the time, I do. For two years I cry myself to sleep almost every night. I have no money, barely manage a single visit in two years to see my kids in England. I see the psychiatrist once a week but always come late. And never know what to say. So I say nothing for the first twenty minutes of every session. After a year, I quit, owing him for practically the full year's sessions.

Divorce. It's terrible. I go into a deep depression. No control whatsoever over my emotions. I'm walking down the street and for no apparent reason start running. Or burst into tears. The separation deeply scars the kids, and that depresses me more. But I've grown up in a home with a contentious marriage. Mel and Renee and I prayed our parents would stop bickering and get a divorce. They did. It just took them twenty-seven years to do it. I feel my ex and I are taking the less damaging route, and our kids will be better for it. It's a tough call but, I hope, the right one.

My children are all pretty mad at me when I leave their mother. Of course. None of them wants the family to break up, and I'm the one doing the breaking. They call me a lot of names, none of them flattering. But here's how they reacted and how they got past it:

Tibby, my first-born, tells me, tearfully, her mother and I will get a divorce. Long before I know it myself. She's very smart, very intuitive. And cute, to boot! Graduates from college, works for Spielberg for six years, goes on to become publisher of *The Venice Paper*. The paper is her passion, and the neighborhood loves her for it. She could run for mayor.

Michael, my eldest son, is fiercely protective of his mother at the time. But he follows me into show business, becomes a very successful producer. He has three fine sons of his own, and he's certainly a much better father than I ever was.

David is studying music on scholarship in England when the breakup occurs. It has to be very confusing for him since he isn't around when the marriage deteriorates. But he works hard at his music, develops into a first-rate classical pianist, gives concerts, lives in Portland, Oregon, but cheers for the Lakers and the Dodgers.

Jennifer is furious about the split, and I don't blame her. But she gets past it, too. She goes into real estate development, becomes the number-one designer and developer in Tucson. Not bad for someone that pretty. And her little son, Bodhi, will one day rule the world!

Nick is only seven when I split. For years, he keeps asking me when I'm coming back to live with them. Very sad, makes me weep. But, to his credit, he gets over it, too, goes on to become an all-American volleyball star, with an MBA from Wharton, and, like his sister Jen, a very successful entrepreneur. Great bunch, eh?

The two mothers-in-law are the least *un*happy with the split. In fact, I'm sure they celebrate it. My mother-in-law was always divisive. Good with her grandchildren, not good with me. She wanted an English nobleman for her daughter, and—surprise, surprise—I wasn't one! And *my* mother—I know she tried to get along with her daughter-in-law. But not very hard, and not for very long. A very good mother, an amazing woman, but she was no cheerleader. The only woman she liked less than my wife was my mother-in-law. Great combo!

Neither of these women broke up our marriage. But, when we did it ourselves, they celebrated. In Henny Youngman's words, "Take our mother-in-laws—please!"

MY FATHER TAKES my divorce the hardest. He had worked so hard to keep his own marriage together—so he's deeply distressed that mine has fallen apart. To him, family isn't the most important thing, it's everything. Especially with kids.

I know he'll be mad when I tell him of the split, and he doesn't disappoint me. He's furious. Eventually, he comes around. Not that he agrees with my breaking up the marriage. But at least he understands that there are valid reasons. That it isn't all on impulse, that I'm not just the crazy kid he always thought I was. Once he understands, he's solidly behind me. Like the good father I always wanted.

It's a very difficult time for all of us. Takes years to recover. But both my ex and I get into better marriages very quickly. And the kids, whom I deeply regret putting through the rough times, turn out remarkably well. They're very resourceful people. Great human beings. I'm proud of each of them, how well they recovered, and what they're doing with their lives.

WHEN I SPLIT up with my wife, Danny Kaye says some things—some very sensitive things—that help me out of my depression. Does he really mean them, or is he trying to console me during my time of sadness? I really don't know. Either way, I can never forget him for it. He makes me feel like a human being again, and here's just the way it happens.

When Herb Bonis calls, it's late that afternoon, summer of '72. I'm in the editing room, wrestling with a couple of *Manhattan Transfer* episodes for CBS.

"Danny would like you to come to dinner."

"Tonight? Impossible."

"No, tomorrow."

"Can't do it, Herb. I've got to deliver by Thursday, and we're way behind." Herb is surprised. I never say no to Danny. "Let Tom edit. He's damn good, and he's faster than you are."

"Herb—I've got to do this one myself. I'm flattered—you know I want to come. He's such a great cook; what's he doing? Chinese?"

"Yeah, Chinese."

"Oh, gawd," I moan. "Herb, I just can't do it. Please, please, thank him for me."

"I'll tell him." He hangs up. But why do I have the feeling I haven't heard the last of it? Sooner or later . . .

Ring, ring . . .

I pick it up. Danny's voice: "Seven o'clock—be on time."

"Danny, I'm editing and . . ."

"Okay, seven-fifteen, no later. It's Bubbles's birthday!" He hangs up.

Oh, gawd. Bubbles is Beverly Sills, his friend, the great soprano, and her birthday is important to Danny. And why didn't I tell him I'm supposed to see my kids tomorrow night, and it's important now that I'm separated from their mother, and they get insecure when I change dates, and now I'll have to start tomorrow's edit at six-thirty in the morning and bring a change of clothes with me and, and, and, and...

... and it's tomorrow night, it's seven-fifteen, exactly, as I ring the doorbell, and Danny comes to the door and lets me in, and I'm wondering why, 'cause his houseman usually does that, but I follow Danny in.

"They're all in there," he says to me, holding my lapel with one hand, as he points to the den door with the other. The door is closed, oddly. Maybe he closed it, who knows?

"They're all in there, and they're talking about you. You know how women talk—yak, yak, yak. Anyway, what they're yakking about is you. How can a man walk out on his family? How can he leave a wife and five kids?"

Danny is doing his impression of women's gossip, and he's doing it very dramatically. And he's talking to me warmly, as a friend would.

"So I told them this—I said, 'Listen, I know Bernie Rothman. He loves his kids very much. So, if he's leaving, he's got a damn good reason to!' That's what I told them, and I wanted you to know." Then he looks me in the eye, and sees I'm crying. "You did the right thing my friend. Not everybody has that kind of guts!"

He turns and walks off.

19

AND

ALL THAT

JAZZ

*M*Y PARTNER AND I PRODUCED A jazz concert at Lincoln Center that was one of the best ever. Won a lot of prizes. And here's why.

We had Duke and the Ellington orchestra, Count Basie and his orchestra, Ella Fitzgerald, Joe Williams, Earl "Fatha" Hines, Dizzy Gillespie, the Dave Brubeck Quartet—on and on. I think we booked every jazz great alive at the time. And with Doc Severinsen hosting, how can we miss? To cap it off, our executive producer, Burt Rosen, managed to reunite the original Benny Goodman Quartet—Benny, Gene Krupa, Lionel Hampton, Teddy Wilson—who hadn't played together publicly since the 1940s, and this was 1972. What a group!

The Duke and I are talking over musical numbers as the band is setting up, and I'm wondering what the hell I'm doing in this lofty company. My partner comes over.

"I hear your son, Mercer, is playing with the band. Which one is he?" Jack asks.

The Duke points to a saxophone player who's handing out sheet music to the other sidemen.

"It's that elderly, dignified-looking gentleman over there."
Cute.

But you gotta know what kind of a thrill it was for me—being there with these icons, listening to them rehearse, talking to them. I had grown up with their music; I was a fan. Now here I am, bossing them around! (That's what producers do.) Telling the great Duke Ellington what I think he should play.

Duke Ellington was the most elegant man I ever met. He had been one of my all-time favorite song writers. I ask him to explain the title of my favorite of his compositions. What did he mean by a Satin Doll? What kind of a woman is she? He thinks this one over, answers in that rich baritone drawl of his. "Well... a satin doll is a lady... who is as soft and warm on the inside... as she is on the outside."

See what I mean—that's elegance!

THEN THERE'S THE business of a show's opening. With all these greats on the bill, what on earth could we go with that was powerful enough to open? An embarrassment of riches. Jack and I decide to pair Ella with the Basie Orchestra and have them do "Lady Be Good." I'd seen them do it before, and it showcased their talent very well. It would set a very exciting tone for the whole evening.

They're both delighted with our nomination. But Bill Basie (the Count) poses a surprising problem.

"Love to do it," he says, "but we don't have an arrangement."

He has to be kidding.

"Nuh-uh. The one you heard us do is an old chart. We need a new one, a hipper one."

I know he's finagling, but figure I can get a new chart for a couple of grand. And it'll be well worth it.

So I call my friend Jerry Toth in Toronto—not only a great arranger but a superb jazz musician in his own right. He can do the job if he's got the time.

"Jerry—I need a big-band chart, and I need it fast. Can you get it to me in a couple of days?"

"Depends," he says. "Who's it for?"

"Ella Fitzgerald and the Count Basie Orchestra."

Long, long silence. "You're kiddin'."

"Nope. They need a new arrangement for 'Lady Be Good.'"

Another pause.

"And how much do I have to pay you to let me write it?"

He stays up all night, and I get it the next day. Count Basie thinks the chart is fantastic, so naturally he asks to keep it when the show is over. And how do you say no to a bona fide count?

MY FIRST MEETING with Ella Fitzgerald is at her home in Beverly Hills. Her secretary, Ms. Atwater, meets us at the door and sits us down in the living room. Moments later, Ella appears. I've admired her for years. (Who hasn't?) She's lost some weight and, because of a recent eye operation, is wearing thick-lensed spectacles. She seems perturbed.

"We're so honored to have you on the show, Miss Fitzgerald," I say, rising.

"Oh no, the honor is mine," she replies with her usual modesty. "You have such an amazing lineup for this show." (Yeah. Like she's chopped liver!)

"Nonetheless..."

"But I'm very upset," she says. "I've just come from my doctor, and he tells me I'm going to have to wear these glasses on stage."

"And that upsets you?"

"Of course it does. How will my fans recognize me?"

Sweet lady, they'll manage, I think. No one will mistake you for Dave Brubeck!

Last thing you see on our concert stage is Ella, wearing those glasses, dancing the jitterbug with Dizzy Gillespie. And her fans *do* recognize her.

THE '30S AND '40S were known as the "swing era," and Benny Goodman was known as the "King of Swing." He was a classically trained clarinet player who had somehow learned to play the syncopated rhythm that was natural to jazz players.

Nobody could beat eight-to-the-bar better than Benny Goodman. No one could beat it faster than Benny. No one had a better feeling for swing. Not only was his big band amazingly popular, but Benny spun off a quartet that was one of the most amazing aggregations in the history of jazz. It consisted of drummer Gene Krupa, vibes player Lionel Hampton, Teddy Wilson, a great "glide" piano player, and of course, the King himself.

The one thing that all his sidemen have in common is that they all hate Benny. Well—maybe not *hate*. But he's a tough taskmaster, with a cold personality. After decades of playing with Hampton, Benny still can't get his name right. Keeps calling him Larry instead of Lionel. Lionel has no problem with names. He just calls Benny "boss" and everyone else "buddy." Benny continually browbeats Krupa: "You're draggin', Gene!" Bull! Krupa has the steadiest tempo of any drummer I've ever heard. It's just Benny keeping Gene in line, showing him who's boss. And poor Teddy Wilson—Benny keeps yelling out chords for him to play. Teddy knows what chords to play, but he also knows never to answer Benny back or the tyranny will become crueler. Then, secretly, he starts drinking in his dressing room. By the time we find out, Teddy has shown up drunk for dress rehearsal. We just barely sober him up in time for the show. Benny is furious, but we don't care. Now we understand why they haven't played together for thirty years.

THE GOODMAN QUARTET rehearses three numbers for six weeks. They play all three flawlessly, but that's all they play flawlessly. The plan is to perform two of the three numbers, save the last for an encore. Doesn't happen that way.

We place Benny's group way down in the program—more of a sentimental item than a band to compete with Basie or Ellington or even Brubeck. Mistake! The Benny Goodman Quartet stops the show cold! They open with "Avalon," a real upbeat number. Standing ovation. Then a slowish ballad—"Moonglow"—figured we'd cool 'em down. Gorgeous. Another standing ovation. Then, "Ding Dong Daddy from Dumas"—hot stuff—so hot the audience won't let them leave the stage. I count seven curtain calls, long and loud—with the audience on its feet. Finally, the quartet gives in—they'll do one more encore. Which they do, and wish they hadn't. Unrehearsed since 1943, it's a disaster. But the audience keeps on cheering and cheering. What a night!

{ **20** }

S H E

G A V E M E

F E V E R

*S*O THERE I AM, HAVING DRINKS with Peggy Lee. Talk about living your fantasies—it's late at night in her dimly lit living room, the music's playing. She pours us enough Scotch to take a bath in. (I hate Scotch, love baths!) I'm sitting on a pink velvet sofa next to my favorite female vocalist of all time, wondering who the hell I think I am. I'm with *Peggy Lee*, that's who I am! She's in her late fifties now, light blonde, and still pretty. The blue velvet gown she's wearing isn't sexy; she's what's sexy. Without even trying. And me with my jacket off, my feet up on her coffee table—real intimate. But it's not a love affair—just feels like one. No, it's like a scene from a '40s movie.

But it's the early '70s, and I'm here to pitch the still-at-her-peak Miss Peggy Lee a one-woman special for Canadian TV. The show's about men, whom, I suspect, the woman loves, if not too wisely, then too well. She's not at all what I expected. The "Hard Hearted Hannah" persona is a fake. She's warm, she's soft, she's vulnerable, she's a pussycat. She doesn't talk;

she purrs. And she's the only person in the music business who has good things to say about Benny Goodman:

"Look—he gave me my first break. I was a kid, singing in a dive in Chicago. He heard me, he liked me, he hired me. I traveled with his band for three years and never had an argument. He looked after me like a father."

I'm dubious: "Boy, that sure isn't 'the book' on Benny."

"Maybe not," Peggy says. "I know he gets bad-mouthed a whole lot. But the man's a genius—you can learn from him. And a lotta guys did."

We talk about the old days—on the road with the big bands. "A girl could grow up real fast." There was Tommy Dorsey's band, Woody Herman's, Harry James's, Count Basie's, Glenn Miller's—all the greats. And the vocalists who traveled with them—Helen Forrest, Martha Tilden, Ray Eberle, the Modernaires. She has warm words to say about all of them. Well, almost all of them...

"It's very sad to me," Peggy says, with real compassion. "Pussy, being the wonderful thing that it is, that three of them were wasted on the Andrews Sisters."

That's what she says. Honest. Then she puts on a record.

"It's my new LP," she says. "They're thinking of releasing this next cut as a single. Tell me what you think."

It's a very unusual song. Different from anything she's ever sung, but Peggy makes it her own. And as she sings, my head begins to spin:

Is that all there is?
Is that all there is?
If that's all there is, my friend,
Then let's keep dancing...

This is not your run-of-the-mill pop song. It's very

cynical—like that expressionistic stuff Kurt Weill and Berthold Brecht wrote in postwar Germany. (Actually, it was two brilliant songwriters from Chicago, Jerry Lieber and Mike Stoller, who wrote it. They also wrote several of Elvis Presley's greatest hits. Talk about range!)

Peggy finishes. I'm convinced the record is going to be a smash and tell her so. But something is bothering me.

"Do you really believe that?" I ask her.

"Believe what?"

"Those words—you really believe life is empty—'that's all there is'?"

Takes her a moment, then she laughs a raucous laugh, raises her glass up high and bellows, "Hell, no!"

And that's all there was.

above: Dad, Mom, and three budding superstars

below: My dear friend Cohen and his dear friend Anjani

above: The fabulous
Art Carney, for once
without Gleason

right: Christopher
Plummer, who hosted
Ottawa for me

above: Vincent Price—the elegant "horror" star

below: Four snow-jobbers—Ferrier, Tadman, Bert Convoy, and me

top left: Brilliant Danny Kaye—the last of the big-time gypsies

bottom left: Roy Clark and his two little piggies

above: Duke Ellington, actually listening to me

above: The incredible flying Nureyev

top right: Zsa Zsa darling and me, darling

bottom right: Gene Kelly—the greatest of all charmers

above: Two great divas—Shari Lewis and Lamb Chop

below: Carl Reiner—in a golden age, he did it all

21

DANNY KAYE—

WITH AND

WITHOUT HIM

*D*ANNY KAYE WAS BASICALLY A KIND man, but sometimes he could be testy and stubborn. People expected him to be the sensitive, charming personality he played on screen. But if he didn't feel like it, he was a bear. I guess that's what years of therapy will do for you. Frees you from living up to other people's expectations. I had no personal expectations of Danny—just professional ones. Which he invariably lived up to. I always told him the truth. Not always easy.

So when Danny asks me to write him a song for the CBS affiliates' show, I know he's going to be in a bad mood. He doesn't really like "the Suits," but it's part of his deal. Also, he doesn't like the show's director, who he thinks is a kiss-up (he's right). By the time I get there to teach him the song, he's already alienated the entire studio. He tells the director he's only going to give him one take. Bluntly. The director pleads—it's a complicated number; he needs time. "Take all the prep time you need," says Danny, "but you're only getting one shot at it." Ridiculous, I think. He'll change his mind.

Twenty minutes later, the director signals he's ready to roll, and Danny performs the number. A mediocre performance.

"Did you get that?" Danny calls out to the director.

"Yes, but Danny . . ."

"That's it," our hero yells. "That's a wrap!"

Danny walks off the stage and over to me at the piano. "How was I? Pretty rotten?"

"Worse," I deadpan, sure that he'll do it over.

"If I wasn't such a stubborn bastard I'd do it again, wouldn't I?"

"Uh-huh." Still sure.

He smiles, pinches my cheek, and walks out of the studio.

He *was* a stubborn bastard, wasn't he? He easily could have obliged. But maybe he had a hot date, who knows?

DANNY KAYE LOVES his work and loves working. He is a quick study and never tires of rehearsing—that's what makes him such a polished performer. But like I say, he's stubborn. When he doesn't want to rehearse, nothing can induce him to. And such is the case in the middle of the rehearsal period for "Danny Kaye's Look-In at the Metropolitan Opera." I'll give him this: he warns me in advance: "I'm taking off Tuesday, Wednesday, and Thursday next week. Don't expect me in." No explanation.

I'm worried. Not for him—like I said, he is a quick study, and he'll be letter perfect. But for the rest of the cast— Beverly Sills, Robert Merrill, and the other opera stars. I've written a pretty complex ensemble piece for them, a medley combining a dozen or so of opera's most famous themes. I've called it "Tops in Ops," and Danny is central to it. The others need him there to rehearse. Because although they are all great voices, showbiz isn't exactly their cup of tea.

And there is something else. Alone in New York without an agenda for three whole days is a death sentence for me. I have no friends there—what am I going to do—go to the movies for three days? Stay in my hotel room? My marriage has just broken up, and I hate being alone. So I call Bobbi.

Bobbi was my summer camp sweetheart when I was sixteen. Great girl! I saw her a couple of times during college years. But she was a New Yorker, I lived in Montreal, so she classified me as G.U.—Geographically Undesirable. Too bad. If we'd lived in the same town, maybe Bobbi would have been the first Mrs. Rothman. But at this time, I have neither seen nor spoken to her in twenty-three years. Now what sane and sober person picks up a phone and calls an old sweetheart he hasn't spoken to for twenty-three years? Guess!

If only I knew her married name. But maniacs like me don't give up easily. I am reasonably certain that her brother is still using his maiden name. And since New Yorkers never leave New York, he's probably listed in the New York directory.

He is. And he remembers me. Carl and I talk for an hour before I ask about Bobbi. Yes, she's been married, has three kids, divorced a few years ago, and is seeing a guy. Awwww, I think—something I often think. But Carl gives me his sister's number, and I call it right then and there. She answers, I recognize her voice.

"Bobbi?"

"Yes, this is Bobbi."

"Bobbi, you may not remember me, 'cause it's been a long time..."

"Bernie Rothman?"

How'd she guess? Hadn't even talked Canadian. And, no, Carl couldn't possibly have tipped her off.

We talk warmly, endlessly on the phone—everything

that's happened to us over the last twenty-three years. So, already, the first night of my three-day sentence in New York turns out fine. Then I ask her out to dinner.

"Can't, Bern. I'm seeing someone."

A second "awwww," louder than the first.

"How about lunch tomorrow?" she suggests, and my second day without Danny is taken care of. She wants to look me over at lunch. Women!

SO WHAT'S SHE like? Adorable. Just like you figured, right? Summer camp sweethearts are always adorable, so why wouldn't Bobbi be? Still very pretty, very warm, very brunette, very smart, very well dressed, full figured in a very pale pink Chanel suit. Very, very, very lovely woman. Has she changed? Of course she's changed, I hear you thinking. She's more grown up, more serious, more sure of herself. Wrong on all counts. Bobbi has always been very grown up, very sure of herself. Everything that I'm not. So while I was struggling to navigate the savage jungle they call the Entertainment Industry, Bobbi was learning that even if you do everything right, which she usually does, a marriage could go on the rocks. And hers did. So Bobbi has become more vulnerable, while I have become less vulnerable. We meet in the middle.

We're perfectly at home with each other that sunny spring afternoon, lunching al fresco at the Ginger Man. Happy to be together, chatting, laughing, gossiping through the years.

"It's just New York," I say, washing down my scrumptious hamburger with a mouthful of California cabernet. "I could never live here."

"And I could never leave it," says the lady, carefully picking at her salade niçoise. (No wonder she still has that figure.)

"Why not?" I ask, innocently enough, but we both know we're laying the groundwork for future negotiations. Just in case!

"There's no other city like it. New York has everything—theater, museums, restaurants, shopping, culture, excitement—everything!"

"Everything but livability," I say. "You've got to come to the Coast for that!"

"You don't know New York," she tells me. "If you knew it as we New Yorkers do, you'd love it."

"Maybe..."

"Come to dinner tonight. My parents will be there; they'd love to see you again."

Yeah, right, your parents! "That's very nice of you."

"Steve's coming, too. You'll like each other."

Fat chance. "You sure?"

"I'm sure. Ulterior motive. I'm going to change your mind about New York."

She never does.

BOBBI'S PARK AVENUE condo is a miracle in good taste: beautiful signed French antiques, fine paintings on every wall, and a rococo fireplace that burns hard dry wood that crackles as it fills the air with musty perfume.

I bring a bottle of Pommard, with a note about the first time I'd tasted that particular Burgundy. It's an intimate note. Thankfully, Bobbi doesn't open it.

Bobbi's folks—good solid people—just as I remembered them. The boyfriend—oh, I don't know—a nice enough fellow, obviously in love with Bobbi, or is he? But I remember thinking: she's mine.

Dinner is warm and friendly. With a baked chicken and artichoke dish—delicious. We don't drink my wine, but the conversation is good, if uncontroversial, and we all get along. Ends early.

Soon after I get back to my hotel, Bobbi calls. It's midnight. She's read my letter.

"You're very special," she says. Takes my breath away.

Why had I waited twenty-three years to hear her say it?

THIRD DAY. NOT going so well. Trying to get some work done. Can't get my mind off Bobbi. Call to thank her for the evening. She enjoyed it, too. No, I haven't changed my mind about New York.

She and Steve are going to theater tonight. Damn! Haven't knocked him out of the box yet.

Ring, ring. Ben Vereen's manager. Ben's playing the Waldorf tonight. Would I come see him? Catch his show and maybe we'll put a deal together to produce his summer series for NBC. What do I want—the ten o'clock show or the midnight? I take the midnight, 'cause already I've got an idea.

Later. Ring, ring, ring. She answers.

"Bobbi, is that you?"

"Uh-huh. Just got in from theater. What's up?"

"I've gotta go see Ben Vereen at the Waldorf tonight—wanna come?"

Pause. "Bernie, it's quarter to eleven."

Pause. "I knew you'd say that."

I hang up. I've baited the trap. Jump into the shower.

Ring, ring.

Dripping wet: "Hello."

"Gimme twenty minutes; I'll meet you in the lobby."

It worked!

I'M WAITING AS she makes her entrance into the Waldorf lobby in a stunning Balmain coat. Knockout! Upstairs, Ben's show is real good. We're old friends, so he plays to me and to Bobbi. He's sexy, and that never hurts. And after the show he comes over, has a drink with us. Very charming. Wants me to produce his summer show. (NBC eventually goes with someone else.) Makes me look good!

Then we go home. Bobbi and I. Together. To her house. And that's the end of the third day without Danny. And the first day of Bobbi and me. We're in love. Beautiful!

THREE MONTHS LATER, we're in New York. But I don't mind, 'cause I'm nominated for an Emmy Award for "Danny Kaye at the Met." We drive up to Lincoln Center for the televised awards show—Bobbi and I, in a limousine. Cheering crowds. It's terrific! I win my first Emmy—and Bobbi.

IT TAKES TWO and a half years for Bobbi to move out to California. At one point, I break off the relationship, because she won't make up her mind. Of course she has her reasons—she's deeply rooted in New York life, has three kids in school there, lots of friends and family in the area—all good reasons. Still, I have to make a life for myself, if not with Bobbi, then with someone. I don't think we would have made it without the help of our kids.

Between us, we have eight kids—one for each teen year and one for good luck. (Now there's a Hanukkah nightmare for you!) And they really like each other. Maybe not right away, but soon, gradually. So what often breaks up second marriages turns out to be a strength in ours. For instance, I don't know if Bobbi ever would have moved to L.A. if her daughter, Ellen, hadn't moved here first. Ellen likes the informal lifestyle of the West Coast. Suits her artistic temperament. She and I become friends early on. Likewise, she gets close to my eldest two, Tibby and Michael, maybe because they're the three parental kids. Or maybe they just have good taste and like each other. My Nick and Bobbi's Andrew have lots in common—they're both the youngest in their families and the hardest driving. Two intense MBA types, just as competitive on the tennis court as they are in the boardroom. Of course, Andrew's older brother, the laid-back Jimmy, easily whops both of them on the court but always lets his stepfather win a few games out of kindness. My Jen has a lot in common with Bobbi—they're city girls and major shoppers. David, my middle child, a talented musician, may be the loner in the family, but he never forgets a sibling's birthday. And yes—eight is definitely enough!

All my kids love Bobbi. And really respect her. And I've never had anything but loving kindness from Bobbi's three. So when we finally elope after seven years living together (Bobbi's mom refers to me as her sin-in-law), our kids are not only thrilled but a bit relieved.

"It's about fucking time!" says Andrew when we phone him with the news.

So, I dunno—are we a blended family? Yup!

22

THE

HALLS OF

FAME

*T*WO BEAUTIFUL WOMEN: BOBBI AND my Emmy Award. I stumble through my short acceptance speech to a national TV audience, petrified. My speech to myself takes a little longer. I congratulate myself, tell myself there'll be more Emmys, but remind myself that Emmys don't make you money. Producing and packaging do.

It's famed songwriter Sammy Cahn who gets Rothman/ Wohl Productions into the packaging business. Sideways. Packaging, in showbiz parlance, means putting a show together, creating it, owning it, and licensing it for broadcast. Not necessarily in that order. It's what everyone in the business wants. Maybe you actually produce the show, maybe you hire someone else to. (I always produce my own shows.) But whatever money's left over from what you received from your licensees is yours. Of course, you've got to pay the cast, the crew—everything comes out of the license fee. Then, you can distribute the show all over the world and make a lot of money. Or lose your shirt!

Sammy, who wrote many of Sinatra's biggest hits, is president of the Songwriters Association of America and asks us to produce their annual Songwriters Hall of Fame Awards show. It's to be staged in the glitzy ballroom at the Beverly Hills Hilton (untelevised) and promises to be a stunning event. A black tie audience is paying two hundred dollars apiece to honor the great songwriters—Harold Arlen, Burt Bacharach, Jimmy Webb, Richard Rodgers—guys who wrote great songs that would be around for decades.

They induct five new composers every year. Each has a celebrity presenter who tells the story of the songwriter's career. Then one of the great singers performs a medley of the writer's hits. This event is a freebie—no one is being paid—not us, not the singers, not the presenters—nobody. But it offers us the chance to work with some pretty hefty performers: Jack Benny, Groucho Marx, Frank Sinatra, Steve Lawrence, Milton Berle, Gene Kelly—an amazing group.

We produce an exciting show. With that kind of lineup, how could we miss? Easy. Just pick the wrong songs or the wrong singer. Berle hosts. He's wonderful to work with, till we start rehearsal. Then he's impossible, insulting, overbearing. When the curtain goes up, he's terrific again. Groucho is hilarious. But, after a long, ambling monologue, we can't get him off stage. Have to send two stagehands out to haul him off stage. But the singers are great, the songs are everyone's favorites, the presenters do their job, and the audience goes home happy. Sammy Cahn likes what we did, and soon word of mouth about our work begins to spread. Visibility's critical in this business.

The best thing we take out of the evening is the format. A model we will use again and again. Each inductee is honored by a different celebrity with his own segment—a mini-special, so to speak. Then comes the presentation. It works. And after all, if the songwriters can have a Hall of Fame, why not the Comedians' Hall of Fame? Or the Musicians' Hall of Fame? Or, for that matter, the Garage Mechanics' Hall of Fame?

The Hall of Fame field is wide open. No one is honoring "life's body of work" in those days. And you don't need an actual hall, just an imaginary one, where the best in any endeavor can be honored for their life's body of work.

So it happens that we produce our first package: "The Horror Hall of Fame." We sell it, or rather, license it to ABC's Wide World of Entertainment. It features horror movies from the very earliest times, starring the earliest film monsters— the original *Phantom of the Opera* and *The Golem, Dracula,* right up through *Halloween, The Texas Chainsaw Massacre,* and the rest of today's gory bunch.

A little unusual? Maybe. Bit of a spoof? Could be. We get paid peanuts for doing it, but the numbers are good and the show is entertaining. It's hosted by Vincent Price, a horror movie superstar. Vincent does some fascinating interviews with the genre's leading experts, and we show lots of grisly scenes from the great old horror flicks.

Well, it isn't too long before one Hall of Fame leads to another, and before we know it, we're in the big-time packaging business.

Sweet!

I'M A SUCKER for Irish charm. And Gene Kelly should have had his bottled. Or maybe even registered as a lethal weapon.

First meeting is in Gene's living room on Rodeo Drive— Jack and I and our new partner, Johnny Green, MGM's esteemed music director, are there. (We meet Johnny on the *Songwriters* show—he knows everyone in Hollywood.) It's a crisp autumn day in 1973. I remember kicking the fallen leaves on the walk that lead up to Gene's house, because thinking about his dance steps in "Singing in the Rain," I am sure that's what Gene must do every day.

The house is a relatively modest one—red-brick, Georgian, not nearly as imposing as some of its neighbors on upper Rodeo Drive. Inside, it's warm and charming like Gene is, full of art and artifacts. You get the feeling he selected every piece. Nothing fancy—a nice cushy sofa, some overstuffed chairs. But there are paintings on the walls you're pretty sure are French Impressionist. And I don't mean copies.

Up and down the stairs runs Bridget, Gene's pretty midteen daughter. Lots of love between those two. The phone rings—a friend calling from Paris. Gene switches easily into French, but the charm remains Irish.

We're at Gene's, asking, no begging, him to host our awards special. The man is an icon. Perfect to symbolize our Entertainment Hall of Fame. The show has a lofty purpose and a lowly budget. It honors entertainers—five living, five posthumously—"not for what they last did, but for what they did that will last." Good idea, right? Gene seems to like it. ABC has given us a ninety-minute time slot and enough money to fill a Volkswagen's gas tank. The show is legitimate—nominations by a blue-ribbon panel (Leonard Bernstein and Roz Russell are on it), voting by entertainment editors of major newspapers all over the country. We pitch Gene—he's in, he'll host.

We leave happy, send out our first release to the press. The voting begins, gets tabulated by some double-barreled accounting firm, and we've got our ten honorees. They include George Gershwin, Lawrence Olivier, and eight others—they're all great. Again, we're happy. Now we have to persuade the honorees to accept the awards, 'cause there's no point having a Hall of Fame with nobody in it.

First honoree to be tapped is Katharine Hepburn. Johnny knows her well from MGM days. He goes to her house, does a perfect pitch for her to accept the award. "Well, all right, since it's you, Johnny," says the tempestuous Kate. "But I'd much rather be inducted posthumously!" Johnny laughs. "Now where is this big fancy awards show taking place?" Kate wants to know.

Again, Johnny pitches: "MGM has this fabulous new hotel, Kate, with a very glamorous showroom—grandest in Las Vegas. They're pulling out all the stops for us!"

La Hepburn turns purple. "Vegas? You're doing the show in that toilet?"

Johnny quickly backtracks. It's tentative, he says. He leaves with his dignity barely intact.

But now we have a problem. Excuse me—we have two. First, we've got to get out of our contract with the MGM Grand, rumored to be run by the mob. Second, we have to find a new venue. One that costs us no more than the MGM Grand, which we're getting free. Swell!

So I fly to Vegas to meet with the hotel's president, but I take Herb Bonis with me. Herb, as you recall, is Danny Kaye's manager, my mentor, a respected figure in Vegas circles. He's one of the kindest, warmest men alive. Unless you get him mad. Then he's not kind and warm. I mean really, really not!

Happily, the hotel's tough-guy president never gets Herb mad. Herb is calm but deadly serious as he explains that our celebrities are reluctant to make the trip to Vegas. And a show without celebrities will benefit nobody. Makes it sound like we're doing them a favor by pulling out. Brilliant!

Of course, I do my part, too. I sit silently in the corner and tremble. (I do that well.) Till it's over. Then I shake hands warmly. (I'm good at that, too.)

Now for our second problem—where are we going to stage this fabulous event? We have no money. And we need a place Katharine Hepburn won't be ashamed of.

Let me be clear about why money is so important in this case. We own this show. Which means if we spend more than the network gives us, it comes out of our pockets. And there's nothing in our pockets except lint.

Jack comes up with the Hollywood Palladium, a well-known location on Sunset Boulevard. Yes, they want rent money, but for what we're not spending on airfare to Vegas, we can afford the Palladium. Just not much left over for anything else.

So we're out of the woods. Or, so we think, till I get a call from the network executive, who wants to see sketches of our grand scenery.

"No need for sketches, Bob," I tell him, "just a very simple set—platforms, glittery curtains, you know—that way, we can concentrate on our stars." Pure bullshit.

"Glad you've got stars, Bern," he tells me, "but I want to see the sketches." He says this firmly.

Just as firm: "Can't do it, Bob. Not on the money you're paying us."

"We're paying the same money to Smith-Hemion for their show, and they're delivering elaborate sets."

"They're not delivering Gene Kelly, Paul Newman, James Stewart, Carol Burnett..."

Bob interrupts: "Bernie, I'm going to insist!"

Pause. "Then Bob, you're forcing me to invoke my company's rarely used 'SIUYA clause.'"

That stops him: "What's your SIUYA clause?"

And I tell him: "It's our 'Stick It Up Your Ass' clause."

Bob laughs and lets me off the hook. Sometimes being funny helps.

FIRST YEAR THE Entertainment Hall of Fame goes surprisingly well. Paul Newman inducts Tennessee Williams, James Stewart inducts Katharine Hepburn—very unposthumously—Carol Burnett honors the late George Gershwin, and so on. The program runs smooth as silk. In a set that's tastefully simple. Gene is a charming host, introducing the presenters, talking about the honorees. The last to be inducted is Judy Garland, who had left the planet only a few short months previously. Because he and Judy had been such good friends, Gene insists on doing Judy's honors himself. "Knowing Judy was a treat," he says in the final moments. "Working with her was a privilege. Surely, America has produced no finer entertainer." Then he looks up from his script, and into the camera. He can barely get these last, improvised words out. "And you know something, ladies and gentlemen, I miss her very, very much..."

I've got his script. The words are smudged with teardrops.

SECOND YEAR OF the show, we've got two great music directors. Nelson Riddle conducts the orchestra with great flair. And to work with the performers on their musical routines, we have my old friend Ray Charles. No, not the singer Ray Charles. The Ray Charles who was Perry Como's music director for years. Great guy, great musician.

See, what happened was Procter & Gamble was looking for a new TV special, one they could sponsor annually. The guys at Leo Burnett, P&G's Chicago ad agency, saw the show that first year and, to our good fortune, bought it from us for its second year. At six times the price. So we go from no music directors to two in a single year. But nothing in show business ever comes easy.

We find out *our* Ray Charles needs open heart surgery eight weeks before the show. I worry. I worry plenty. Not for the show—we've got a spare music director. But Ray's my friend, and I worry for his life. I'm in the hospital room the night before surgery. His doctor comes in, tells him not to worry—after the operation he'll feel better than he's been feeling for years. Ray turns white. "Doctor, I've been feeling fine, honest. Are you sure I need this operation?"

The doctor's calm. "You'll feel better," he says and leaves the room.

"They're making a mistake," says Ray, alarmed. "I'm sure of it."

Two weeks later, I'm walking the Hills of Beverly for an hour every morning with my friend Ray Charles. Ten days after that, he's back at work. I remember his first day back on the job. Ray's written an elaborate layout of Irving Berlin songs for the great Broadway star Ethel Merman. Ethel had introduced several of the late, great songster's hit songs— "There's No Business Like Show Business," among others— and will induct Berlin into the Hall of Fame. And what a charming woman she is, as I drive her to Ray's house in Trousdale.

The two have never met, but Ray and Ethel have heard about each other for years. They talk and joke like old friends, exchange anecdotes about mutual friends—I'm loving it—just sitting and listening. Then Ray goes over the sheet music with Ethel. It's a medley of three Berlin songs, which Ethel introduced on Broadway. Let's go!

Ray sits down at the piano. Ethel, sheet music in hand, leans into the vortex of the piano like a nightclub singer. I sit on a stool, four feet away from her, so that I can hear every note. I needn't have.

The music starts, and Ethel gives out with a flawless chorus and a half of Irving Berlin's "There's No Business Like Showbusiness" and she's singing at the top of her lungs, just like on the Broadway stage, full volume, so every member of the audience can hear her thirty rows back. No need for a mic. She'll knock 'em dead!

And she does. She's one of a dozen top performers, including Jack Lemmon, Ben Vereen, Anthony Newley, Sandy Duncan, Ginger Rogers, and Henry Fonda, who all knock 'em dead at our gorgeously decorated Hollywood Palladium that night. And Kelly is fantastic! He's everywhere—talking, singing, joking, and yes, even dancing on our stage. The audience loves it, the reviews are ecstatic, critics are calling it the best awards show on the air. Rothman/Wohl gets a pickup for our third year of *The Entertainment Hall of Fame*. We're flyin'!

OUR HONOREES ARE amazing! Ever wonder what Fred Astaire was really like? Could anybody be that suave, that sophisticated, that charming? Answer: yes. Add one more adjective: modest.

I spent only ten minutes in his company. Mr. Astaire was one of our five great living artists being inducted into the Entertainment Hall of Fame. He had accepted our invitation to visit the set that afternoon so we could show him around.

When he arrived, I introduced myself as the show's producer and took him on a tour of the theater—where to make his entrance, where Gene Kelly would introduce him, where Ginger Rogers would present him with his award, and so on. He seemed genuinely enthusiastic. As we finished, he became pensive.

"You know, Bernie," he said, "I was thinking—when I woke up this morning—I'm seventy-nine years old. I first appeared on stage when I was five. That's seventy-four years I've been an entertainer—loved doing it. And now I'm being inducted into the Hall of Fame." He shook his head in disbelief. "Wow! I'm a lucky guy."

He shook my hand and disappeared out the door. Gracefully.

THE SHOW IS a success, but the ratings are a disappointment. They're okay, but just okay. NBC expected more. P&G did too. So we go into our third year with a little less momentum than we'd hoped for.

Still, we've got a highly prestigious show, the full support of the trade, and best of all, we've got a phenomenal host in Gene Kelly. Or do we?

We have Gene Kelly till the morning his agent calls to tell us we don't. What happened? What could possibly have happened for Gene to pull out less than a month before the show? Was it the money? Was it health? Was he unhappy with us in any way?

No, no, and no, Gene tells us, when we speak to him at his home that day. It's a freak thing, a one-in-a-million freak thing. We had scheduled the show on his daughter's high school graduation day. He had promised Bridget to be there, and with Gene, a promise is a promise. Too late for us to change the date of the show. And he's not going to renege on his promise. So there we are; we need a new host.

We get three of them. Art Carney, Diahann Carroll, and Leigh Grant. Three fabulous performers with talent, humor, poise. Leigh is an actress with great stage presence. Diahann is beautiful, a great singer. And Carney, a veteran comedy star, has always been America's favorite. We got it made.

As good as our troika is, the three of them don't add up to one Gene Kelly. The performances are there, but the spirit of the show—the true Hollywood spirit—is gone. The ratings sink to below acceptable. The show is off the air.

I WAS GOING through some old letters the other day when I found one from Gene. It was a thank-you note for the bottle of champagne we'd sent him after it was all over.

"Dear Guys," it said. "Thanks for the contraband. You are gentlemen of the old school. One day, you'll be gentlemen of the new. Warmly, Gene."

Warmly, indeed!

IF ALL THIS looks like a piece of cake to you, you need glasses! I don't know anyone in entertainment who'll tell you he or she has had an easy time. That includes the biggest and the best. Ask Steven Spielberg if he's had an easy time. What was it like after his movie *1941* bombed? Ask Michael Eisner what it's been like dealing with the Disney board. Or Tom Hanks or Jack Nicholson or Barbra Streisand—ask them how easy their climb up the ladder was.

One good show doesn't lead to another—you've always got your back against the wall. So why does it sound like so much fun? 'Cause it is. It's exciting, it's creative, it's a million laughs. And if you're going to survive, you'd better think positively. The good times can turn into bad ones; the lucky streak doesn't last forever. It's fun, it's exciting, but it sure ain't easy. Ask anyone who's been there.

So after three seasons of producing our highly visible, very prestigious awards show and hobnobbing with many of the greatest stars of the day, I am confident my career will take off. After all, the networks know us now, know they can trust us to deliver top-quality shows. We expect our phone to ring. It doesn't.

I remember hearing stories about how difficult it was for *Laugh-In*'s brilliant creator/producer, George Schlatter, to sell NBC a follow-up show. After delivering that runaway hit that soared over the ratings for nearly a decade and changed the face of television, he was facing a stone wall on the next one. Same story for Danny Arnold, who was the one-man show for the life of a ten-year run for the *Barney Miller* series, one of ABC's most successful sitcoms ever. But he had a hard time launching his next one, and it never really got off the ground. What is it, I wondered, about these guys? Did success go to their heads?

In retrospect, I don't think so. Such is our business that whether your last show was a success or a failure, you're starting from scratch when it's all done. And that's what keeps driving us in this business—your last show could well have been your *last* show.

SO AFTER *Hall of Fame,* we go back to the networks. We develop comedy series for them, dramas, musicals, MOWS (movies-of-the-week), but nothing goes past the development stage. And whereas a writer can make a decent living writing pilot scripts, a producer can't. After eight months of nothing but development, I'm beginning to despair.

23

WELCOME

TO THE

BIG TIME

*T*HE NETWORKS AREN'T COURTING US, but Procter & Gamble is. They encourage us, sponsor us, and promote our work, and through their advertising agencies, they're always open to fresh ideas. And that's something my partner and I have an unlimited supply of.

It's research that decides us to do *Pinocchio*. Carlo Collodi's classic morality tale about a troublesome puppet who wants to be a real boy had been published in more languages than any other book in the history of print. Except the Bible. That's what decides us. The Disney animated version had been immensely successful. But that was years before. No "live-action" version had ever matched that success. So we decide to try.

We sell this original yet-to-be-written live musical with perfect casting. The adorable dancer/actress Sandy Duncan will star in the title role—a puppet who comes to life and wants to be a real boy. Sandy has a refreshing tomboy quality, and heaven knows, she can move like a puppet. Danny

Kaye will play the role of Gepetto, the old Italian wood carver who created the puppet. Danny has a true affinity for the role, and he's every inch an international superstar. That's how we sell the show to CBS. That's how we sell it to P&G, who back us all the way. Perfect!

Herbie Baker is writing the script—we all have faith in him—and our choice for the score is a brilliant new songwriter, Joe Raposo. Joe made his name writing excellent songs for *Sesame Street* ("It's Not Easy Being Green") and some fine ballads for Frank Sinatra. Since we want a score that's catchy enough for kids but sophisticated enough for grown-ups, he sounds just right. So we hire Joe.

Six weeks into pre-production we have three-quarters of a script. It's awfully good. But where are the songs, Danny's manager, Herb Bonis, wants to know. So do I. We've had nothing from Mr. Raposo. We talk every day and he stalls every day. He makes vague promises over the phone (he lives in New York), but no music shows up. What's going on with him? Out of desperation, I fly to New York and camp at his studio, while he sits at the piano, painfully picking out tunes. Ten days later, he gives me a cassette with three songs on it. One of them is good. When I get home, I send the cassette to Danny. Half an hour later, Herb calls to tell me: Danny's off the show. Which is like hearing the warm-up sound of the guillotine!

I think hiring Billy Barnes to pinch-hit for Joe Raposo was my idea. But it might have been Jack's or Herb's. Billy is a very skilled Broadway-style songwriter. We'd worked together on Danny's series, and, truthfully, we should have hired him in the first place. So I fire Joe and hire Billy. Danny loves the idea, and my career gets a reprieve—Danny's back in. As Jack puts it, "Ya gotta be made of steel in this business!"

Danny and Sandy are unforgettable in their roles. Virtuoso turns, with remarkable chemistry. There's gossip on set that they're involved, but it's nothing like that. Just good acting. And singing. And dancing. Danny, with that finely tuned ear of his, brings the fatherly old Italian to life. And Sandy—all she has to do is move, and the woman becomes a puppet who becomes a little boy. Bill Hargate's costumes are so vibrant and colorful they easily rival the Disney version. Billy Barnes writes a delightful score—"I'm Talkin' to Myself Again," the lonely old Gepetto sings, longing for a son. "What's That?!" sings Pinocchio, as he comes to life, sees all the magic creatures in the town square for the first time. And Ron Field's staging brings Broadway sophistication to the charming children's fable. Australian actor Clive Revill plays the coachman—a villain that could scare you out of your worst case of hiccups. Stan Winston's masks for Flip Wilson and Liz Torres as the Fox and the Cat are as wildly eccentric as the animals they're playing. The show is a colossal success. We get five Emmy nominations, rave reviews, and huge ratings, and we sell the show in thirty-seven countries around the world. That's a lot of countries! It's still running in many of them. Hey—sometimes you get lucky.

NEXT YEAR, WE do a follow-up, 'cause CBS wants one. So does P&G. So they talk us into it. (Takes 'em maybe three minutes.) Ergo: *Once Upon a Brothers Grimm.*

No Danny Kaye, no Sandy Duncan, but instead Dean Jones and Paul Sand, two excellent actors. They might not have the drawing power we had for *Pinocchio,* but they are certainly two men who can carry a musical. Dean has starred in a number of Disney movies, sings well, is very accomplished in the family entertainment field. Paul, playing the younger of the two Grimm brothers, is as charming as can be and gives an impishness to the kid brother character. There's a host of cameo players—Teri Garr, Arte Johnson, Sorrell Booke, Ruth Buzzi, and loads more—a fine script by Jean Holloway (not as funny as Herb Baker's for *Pinocchio,* but it's written beautifully), and a score by Sammy Cahn and Broadway's Mitch Leigh (*Man of La Mancha*). Plus twice the budget we had for *Pinocchio.*

Sound like a powerful show? Should do better than last time, right? Well it doesn't. And stupidly, we overspend our budget thinking we can make the money back on the next one. We're sure there will be a next one. And a few more after that. We're the only ones doing these lavish musicals, and we did so well on our *Pinocchio* we're confident they'll order a whole bunch more. Wrong!

We learn that the more the buyer gives you, the more he expects back. We end up a quarter of a million bucks in the hole.

JACK AND I are at our accountant's office. Panic time.

"It's very simple," says Jay Gilman, our CPA. "You've got no money, you owe these guys a fortune, and you've got nothing coming up to pay them with."

"So what are you saying?" says Jack.

"Declare bankruptcy," says Jay. "You got no choice."

"You agree with that, Bern?" says Jack.

"Nuh-uh," say I. "I didn't get into this business to go bankrupt."

"C'mon, guys," says Jay. "You gotta take the plunge— start out fresh. You'll get your company back in two or three years."

Couldn't do it. Wouldn't do it. Didn't do it.

FOR THE NEXT three years, we use every nickel we earn to pay back our creditors. We take every job we can—sometimes two at a time—but we do it. One day, we get a call from our biggest creditor, the Goldwyn Studios. They've just received our last pay-back check, and the controller wants to take us to lunch. Which they do. The Goldwyn finance team is very flattering. They admit they never expected to see the money back.

"We need one favor," the controller says. "Promise that if anyone ever asks you for a credit reference, you'll send him to us."

And we did. Often. And never got turned down for credit the rest of our company's life.

BROTHERS GRIMM WAS one of the great disappointments of my producing days. My partner and I put everything into it—money, hours, production values—and we figured we'd have a hit. But we didn't. The script was well written, but it was too lyrical—not funny enough. The aesthetics were there—the costumes, the sets, the corps de ballet—but the pace was slow—languid, in fact. I should have done a tighter job of editing. And even with excellent individual performances, the chemistry wasn't there. The magic was missing. The show was certainly not a flop (it received four Emmy nominations), but I expected a great deal more. I did get one wonderful surprise that was worth everything.

My father, who hates my being in show business, never misses my shows. He always calls me afterwards, gives me his own personal critique (usually favorable), then tells me I chose a lousy business, and why on earth am I sticking with it? This time it's different. The closing credits are rolling by when the phone rings. It takes me a while to make out Dad's voice—he's crying. "I finally understand what you see in this business," he says. "That was so beautiful! The music, and the dancing, and the acting, and the costumes..." He goes on and on. But I barely hear him through his tears and mine.

He never again reminds me what a lousy business I'm in.

24

THE TEN

PERCENTERS

I ALWAYS THOUGHT THAT WHEN I got an agent, especially if I was lucky enough to get a good one, my career would take off like a rocket. You write something, he sells it, you pay the guy 10 percent of whatever you make, you keep 90 percent—what could be simpler? Doesn't work that way.

I'm three years into a Canadian writing career and beginning to eye jobs south of the border. So I call my first boss—an amazing director/producer named Norman Jewison—and ask him for recommendations for an agent, 'cause he really knows everything.

"Sure," he says, "two good writers' agencies—I'll call them if you want—Frank Cooper Associates and the Ashley/Steiner Agency."

"Who do you like best?" I ask.

"Both *good, small* agencies, that's what you need. Doesn't matter which one you go with, the day after you sign, call and tell 'em they're not doing their job and you want your papers back."

So I go with Frank Cooper Associates—a *good, small* agency. Next year they merge with Ashley/Steiner, doubling their size. Year or two later they merge again, becoming the Ashley Famous Agency, one of the biggest talent agencies in the world. Doesn't matter. My agent is a guy named Stuart Robinson, and he looks after me no matter what name is on the agency door.

See, it's not the agency that matters, it's the agent. Every agent within the agency has his own clients. That's who he works for. Sooner or later he's going to leave the agency and open his own business, and he hopes that by building your career, he'll have a cash-paying customer to take with him. What I also learn is, the 90/10 ratio is right. You pay them 10 percent of everything you earn, but you do 90 percent of the work.

Your agent can open the door for you, help bolster your career. But an agent can only sell you to people who want to buy. Stuart Robinson is a terrific agent. But there are plenty of times when buyers are in short supply, and you wonder if you'll ever work again.

THE JOB OF an agent is to solicit work for you and negotiate your deals. The job of a manager is to strategize your career and ride herd on your agent. An agent can only commission 10 percent of what you get. By law. A manager can take any percentage you're willing to pay him. Could be 50 percent.

Bernie Brillstein is a brilliant manager, guided the careers of John Belushi, Chevy Chase, Lorne Michaels, and many others. His colleague, Sandy Wernick, guided Rothman/ Wohl Productions for a number of years. Most of his clients are producers, directors, and writers. He has a knack of digging things up—getting on the phone every morning, talking to network people, studio people, packagers—finding out who needs what so he can fill their needs with his clients. An excellent manager is Wernick, who helped develop Rothman/Wohl into a truly creative production company, with an excellent reputation, and a great many award-winning shows to our credit.

THE BEST AGENT in the world is Mike Ovitz. And everybody knows it. He makes more deals, better deals, for more people and for more money than anyone before or since. Mike Ovitz is an irresistible force.

He's a junior agent at the William Morris office when I meet him in 1970. Most of the senior agents are petrified of him. They know how good he is. And how relentless. A few years later, Mike leads a pack of his young colleagues out of the Morris Agency, forms CAA—the Creative Artists Agency—which develops into the most powerful talent agency in the world. Michael is its CEO and is widely regarded as the most powerful man in Hollywood. He controls the careers of Steven Spielberg, Robert Redford, Barbra Streisand, Jack Nicholson, Dustin Hoffman, Meryl Streep, and most of the top movie directors and writers in Hollywood. My experiences with Mike Ovitz leave me with nothing but respect. Besides the toughness, he shows me a compassionate side that I will never forget.

My partner and I are producing a lavish two-hour musical comedy for CBS called *Once Upon a Brothers Grimm*. We hire Ovitz's client Dean Jones to play the lead. Halfway through, we run into production trouble and end up with a quarter of a million dollars' worth of overages. Rothman/Wohl doesn't have that kind of reserve. CAA agent Amy Grossman calls the day after production wraps.

"You paid Dean his first two payments," she says. "The last one is due Thursday—any problem?" I guess she's heard of our troubles.

"Amy, we're a little behind with our bookkeeping," I say. "We may need a few extra few days."

"Oooo, that's serious," she says. "Can you get back to me— Dean needs that money."

I'm worried. Asking for a few extra days isn't out of the ordinary, but there's something in Amy's voice ... I call my banker, make an appointment to come in. I know he'll help— it's a matter of time and timing.

An hour later the phone rings—Amy again.

"Bernie—just speaking to the new partner here. Wants to know when Dean will get his money."

A male voice breaks in. Harshly.

"Bernie, this is Marty Bloom—you know who I am?"

Stunned: "Yeah, Marty."

"Well, if you know who I am, then you know my reputation. The money gets here on time or I call the union and close you down!"

I get off the phone, not knowing what to do. My partner and I talk it over. I'm just leaving for the bank when the phone rings again. It's Ovitz.

"Bernie, Amy just walked out of my office, and I told her she owed you guys an apology. Expect her call. Then I told my new partner if he ever pulls that shit again he'll be my *ex*-partner!" I'm silent. Then Ovitz again: "Bernie, I'm paying Dean what you owe him, and whenever you get the money you can pay me back. If you need a line of credit I'll get you one at my bank. Couple hundred grand enough?"

"Sure, Mike," I say, fighting back tears, "it's enough."

That's how tough Michael Ovitz is.

BEST MANAGER I ever had was Catherine McCartney. Met her in Toronto twenty years ago—she was managing John Candy (whom she'd discovered) and Al Waxman (till the day he died) at the time. She's still with me, a very close friend.

Catherine is welcomed through every door in Canadian television and most of them in the States, too. She cuts a tough deal for her clients, gives nothing but sound advice, smart strategy, and kind consolation. Of course—she's Glaswegian, and did you ever meet a Scot who isn't practical? Beyond that, she's as warm as toast. And you'll never be alone as long as Catherine's with you. Just give her a wee call—you'll find out!

25

INVITATION

TO THE

DANCE

*J*ULIE ANDREWS IS AN ANGEL. OR at least she behaves like one on our CBS *Festival of the Lively Arts* special: warm, charming, intelligent, dependable. Julie loves to dance. So does Rudolf Nureyev. But that's where the similarity ends. Nureyev is past his prime. Still dancing at thirty-eight, he can leap as high as ever, but when he lands—ouch! Maybe that's why he's so impossible to deal with—he's dancing in constant pain. In the end, I earn every nickel of my producer's fee. But his performance is worth it. I believe now as I believed then that the gentleman dancing on our show was the greatest male dancer of the century (sorry, Misha!). But let's start at the beginning.

My partner and I had won Emmys in the mid-'70s for *Danny Kaye's Look-In at the Metropolitan Opera*. Now, six years later, CBS wants a follow-up—something like the opera special—for their *Festival of the Lively Arts* series. What we propose is a special about dance—all kinds of dance, with all kinds of dancers. The show's host will take us through the development of dance—beginning with primitive folk dancing, right up through ballet, Broadway, tap—everything. It takes CBS vice president Michael Ogiens approximately thirty seconds to say yes. And, subject to our finding an acceptable host, this isn't just a development deal; it's a commitment to production. Just find the right host, says Michael. Right!

Julie Andrews is the right host. But how do we get to her? Make an offer through her agent? No chance. Julie's at the peak of her career, no way we can afford her. Manager? Naw. She's a big movie star; why would a manager let her do a television show? Here's how we get her—are ya ready?—through her hairdresser! Julie's hairdresser is also my partner's wife's hairdresser, and that's how we get word to Julie, who loves the idea of hosting a dance show, because Julie *loves* to dance! Now all we need is someone to dance with her.

Rudolf Nureyev is somewhat easier to book because his archrival, Mikhail Baryshnikov, has just done a big TV special, and Rudolf wants to show the ballet world he's still top dog. So we get Rudolf, and we get Broadway star Ann Reinking, hoofer Sandman Simms, Peggy Lyman from the Martha Graham Troupe, the Nashville Cloggers, Rob Iscove's handpicked corps de ballet... shall we dance?

If ever I have memories of a show, this is the one. Starts with our first meeting with Julie. Very gracious lady, impeccable manners. She's warm and receptive as I describe the show to her, item by item. She asks all the right questions, seems satisfied with my answers. Till halfway through the show—she's puzzled by something she reads in the rundown.

"What's this?" she asks.

"What?"

"Number 17—it just says 'something upbeat.'"

"Oh, that," I say. "Haven't quite figured out what to do there. But number sixteen and eighteen are slow, serious numbers, so I figure we need something real hot in between."

She thinks it over. "Well," she says, smiling demurely, "I could always ball the band." Thank you, Mary Poppins.

Listen—maybe she strangles chickens in her attic. But I never spent a moment with Julie Andrews that I didn't enjoy. She's just swell!

RUDOLF IS ANOTHER story. He challenges me every inch of the way. If a producer's to produce, he's got to be the boss. Mr. Nureyev makes that difficult. Oddly, we like each other from the very beginning. He's interesting, well-read, intellectual. He's even playful at times. I remember watching him in Dostoevsky's *The Idiot* as an enthralled audience jumped to its feet with a tumultuous ovation at the end. They gave him eleven—count 'em, eleven—curtain calls. After the fifth I left my seat and went backstage to watch his bows from the wings. As the applause died down, Rudolf pranced offstage, came at me, kissed me on the mouth, and said, "How vas I?" Was he kidding? Ten minutes of bravos and curtain calls and he wants to know how he "vas." I think he knew how he "vas." He vas fabulous! He just wanted to hear me say it.

At times he was cruel. On more than one occasion I saw him make his prima ballerina cry. He was known for destroying his dance partners—nagging, demanding, deriding, criticizing. I began to understand his cruelty when, one evening, a bit tipsy from the bubbly (his favorite drink was champagne—made him an expensive date), he told me about his dad. His father was a colonel in the Russian army and was a very stern man. When Rudolf told him he had chosen ballet for his career, his father beat him. And beat him every night, mercilessly, until Rudolf finally ran away from home.

"That's vy I am great dancer!" he told me proudly. And he certainly was. He was the greatest.

WE'RE STAGING THE show at the Merriweather Post Pavilion, just outside Washington, D.C. We expect an audience of four or five thousand people, including senators and cabinet members and their families. (CBS wants brownie points.) We rehearse at the Minskov Studios during an oppressive heat wave in New York City. Murder!

But that isn't the only reason we're sweating. The pressures are unbelievable. The show itself is shaping up, but every day Rudolf is becoming more difficult.

It's during rehearsal, three days before the show, that he calls me aside.

"I've been thinking," he says, somewhat ponderously, "this is show about dance. I am dancer. Julie is singer. Vy she is getting top billing?"

I can't believe my ears! "Rudolf," I say, looking him straight in the eye, "you and Julie are both big stars. But Julie was on the show first. This was all negotiated and settled with your manager months ago."

"Perhaps," he says. "But I am star of dance, she is singer. I must get first billing."

I just stare at him. He stares back. "I am in very self-destructive mood," he says, scowling. "I vould not vant to valk out on you on day of show!"

Is that a threat? Three days before the show and my star is threatening to walk? Disaster!

I call Mike Ogiens at CBS, tell him what's going on.

"Fire the fucker!" Mike says, with dispatch.

"Mike—it'll leave a big hole in the show."

"So get someone else. I'll have our people help you. And if we need to postpone, we'll postpone."

God bless Ogiens, always there for us.

Now I have to let Julie know. Call her agent, give him the whole story. Promise I'll stand by her top billing clause. But we *could* lose Nureyev. The agent promises to talk to Julie and call me back in an hour. He calls back in ten minutes.

"Julie says she loves the show and loves you guys. If you need to give him the billing, go ahead. She'll stand by you any way you want."

Like I said—the woman's an angel.

Now Gorlinsky, Rudolf's agent.

"Sandor—your client's acting up. Wants to change the billing clause that you and I negotiated months ago. Gonna have to let him go."

Long silence. Followed by a very nervous Gorlinsky saying: "I'll talk to him. Don't do anything brash."

So I don't. Next morning, there's Rudolf, all smiles, rehearsing his little dance shoes off. He looks up as I enter. "Good morning, your highness," he says with conciliatory warmth, finishing with a deep bow of humility. Oh, Rudy!

THE PRESSURES MOUNT as we close in on curtain time. The Nederlander people (they own the theater) show up, unannounced, after dress rehearsal, insisting on a renegotiation of the stagehands' contract while they keep a couple of thousand people waiting to be admitted. Jack is enraged by this obvious negotiating ploy. For once, I'm calm. "We're in no rush, Jack," I say in front of the Nederlander group. "I just feel terrible about the millions in damages it's gonna cost our friends here if anything goes wrong." Their side exchange worried glances.

The audience is admitted immediately and the negotiations completed in short order. Surprised? Naw. When in trouble, threaten litigation. Never hurts.

Immediately, a greater problem presents itself. Rudolf has disappeared. Half an hour before showtime, and our star performer is nowhere to be found. Now I'm frantic. I race around backstage, asking everyone, but no one has seen him since dress rehearsal. Then one of the dancers reports she saw Rudolf hurry out, saying he had to go back to his hotel. Disaster! The hotel is a twenty-minute drive from the theater. What possible emergency could have come up? Or was it a spiteful Rudolf, paying me back for giving Julie top billing? I wonder in horror as the hotel operator puts me through to his room. An interminable wait—six, eight, maybe ten rings. Then a male voice that I recognize as Rudolf's masseur, with whom he travels.

"Emil, let me speak to Rudolf," I demand, hoping to be told he's already on his way to the theater.

"Just one moment," he says stiffly. I can hear a heated discussion in the background. Then Rudolf gets on.

"What is it, Bernie?" As if I've rudely interrupted his private life.

I lose it. "What is it? What is it? It's twenty minutes to curtain time and you're half an hour away, that's what it is! What's going on, Rudolf?"

Pause. Then slow and deliberate, "I take bath."

"You what?" I scream.

"I take bath. I am dancer, Bernie. Dancer must take care of body."

"Oh yeah, well you better dance your little body into a cab and get over here, because the show is going on with or without you!"

"I come now," he says without a hint of contrition. "But I must do thirty minutes warm-up before I dance."

"Shorten it!" I command, and hang up.

Then I go to work. Rudolf's first appearance on the show has to be delayed. Which means changing the entire sequence of performances while still maintaining pace and continuity. Jack and I work feverishly on the new sequence, then go to the performers and tell them what has happened and what they've got to do. We get nothing but cooperation. Except from Peggy Lyman, Martha Graham's magnificent lead dancer.

"I won't do it!" she blurts out, firmly, emotionally.

"Peggy, please..."

"Not for that bastard! Never!"

"It's not for him, it's for me, Peggy. And for you and for Martha and for all the dancers on this show."

Eventually, she relents. Not because of anything brilliant I've said, but because she's a nice woman and it's the right thing to do. She explains that Rudolf once appeared with the Martha Graham Troupe and behaved so cruelly, so nastily to all of them—especially dear Martha—that Peggy will never forgive him.

Well, of course, the show goes on. Starts a bit late. Rudolf is ready a little sooner than expected. Performances are outstanding, Julie Andrews is absolutely amazing throughout, and the highlight of the show is a sexy, jazzy duet she does with Rudolf called "I've Got Your Number." Well they certainly got mine. And, I guess, the judges' number, too. They graciously award us another Emmy for the show.

THERE IS A P.S. to this last story. About a year after we do the dance show, the Martha Graham Troupe is appearing in Pasadena, so, of course, I go out to see them. They're fabulous, as usual.

After the show, I go backstage. Much hugging and kissing with Peggy Lyman. We talk, like old friends do, and the remarkable Martha comes over to say hello.

"The show was good," she says. "But I hear Rudolf was nasty."

"He's a bad boy, Martha. Very cruel."

A tear comes to her eye as she says, "And I thought it was just me."

26

THE

SON ALSO

RISES

$\mathcal{W}$ITH THE SUCCESS OF THE DANCE show and our second Emmy in hand, Jack and I are looking for new challenges. One day he gets off the phone and tells me about the story he has just been told and wants us to option. *Son-Rise* is a true story about Raun Kaufman, a little autistic boy, whose family had worked together to cure him of this seemingly incurable children's disease. The boy's father, Barry Kaufman, has written a compelling book in the early '70s about the experience, and several producers before us tried to create a film based on it. All three major networks turned the project down, on the grounds that the story was too internal to make a convincing film. Jack and I disagree. And with some serious input from our creative associate, Molly Miles, we put together a first-rate presentation to show the networks.

We take it to Procter & Gamble, for whom we have produced *Pinocchio* and *Brothers Grimm*. I think they were surprised. Why would they trust a couple of guys who have given them nothing but musical comedies with as serious a subject as autism? But they do.

Together we go to the NBC executives, who must have asked themselves the same question. But they say yes, too. Is it because P&G bought more television time than anyone else in the world? Maybe, maybe not. I think they truly believe in the project, believe we can handle it. Would you? I doubt it. We aren't too sure ourselves. But we get our go-ahead and go ahead. Our first TV movie, our first dramatic film. We are thrilled! And terrified!

NEGOTIATIONS WITH BARRY Kaufman to option his book are long and arduous. He wants final say on the script. Nuh-uh. Final say in casting. Nuh-uh. Wants a guarantee the final script will be his. Nuh-uh. Final say in editing. Nuh-uh. Here's what we tell him. No network in the world will allow anyone final say in anything. Here's what we offer. We'll let him write the first draft. Pay him for it. If we like it, we'll move on to the next. If not, tough! We consult him on casting, editing, and everything else. And nothing in the script will distort the story. We guarantee that. That's all.

His script comes in. Not bad, but not good enough. Plenty of arguing, but we stand on our prerogatives. We'll bring in another writer to rewrite the script. That's when our trouble with the network starts. We want to hire Stephen Kandel, a writer known principally for his action-adventure dramas (*Mannix, Mission: Impossible,* etc.). Not appropriate for this sensitive drama, says the network. Stephen can do it, we say, and stick to our guns. (Stephen is my closest friend. I know him; I know what he can do.) P&G backs us, and Stephen goes on to win the Humanitas Prize, television's most prestigious prize for a writer, for his work on *Son-Rise.*

Because we've never produced this kind of drama before, we bring in Filmways as our partner and Dick Rosenbloom, their finest producer. Dick works with us almost from the beginning. We're also lucky in hiring Glenn Jordan as our director (Dick's nomination). There's no finer director doing movie-of-the-week television. And none tougher.

"What are you doing here?" Glenn asks me that first morning in the studio.

"What d'you mean, 'what am I doing here'? I'm the producer," I say, startled.

"That's not what producers do. They don't come to the studio."

"Really?" I say in my most sarcastic tone. "And what exactly *do* producers do?"

"They go to the 'dailies', give the director their notes, then they go have meetings looking for their next job."

"No kidding," I say. "I've always wondered what producers do."

I never miss a day in the studio, whisper all day long in Glenn's ear. I guess he gets used to my being there. And I certainly value his immense contribution to the production. We become good friends.

Still are.

JAMES FARENTINO AND Kathryn Harrold are our stars. Both very good. But once in a while Farentino's male vanity gets in the way. Like the time I cut one of his favorite scenes out of the film.

"Why'd you cut it?" he asks me. "That was a great scene."

"We were long, and it wasn't necessary to the plot," I say.

Jimmy is pissed because the scene showed him with his shirt off, kind of macho. So he doesn't come to the cast screening of the film. His wife comes.

"My husband's an idiot," she says. "Probably the best thing he's ever done!"

And when he finally sees the show on air, Jimmy agrees.

Sends us a very effusive singing telegram. Good actor, good sport!

One person who *does* make it to the screening is P&G's newly appointed head of production, Jack Wishard. Kind of a hard-nosed guy. But when the lights come up, Jack is rubbing the tears from his eyes. No one ever saw that movie dry-eyed.

Barry Kaufman is another who missed the cast screening. Still resentful about having been replaced as screen writer, he sends a five-page telegram to Fred Silverman, then president of NBC, accusing us of distorting his story in flagrant violation of our contract. He threatens to sue if NBC doesn't make wholesale changes in the film.

Silverman calls us. "Any truth to this?" he asks.

"Not a word," we say.

The show goes on without a single frame changed. Gutsy!

Morning after the broadcast, Barry Kaufman calls.

"Probably the most beautiful piece of work I've ever seen!"

It takes a big man to say that. Tough to see your life portrayed by actors on a screen. And the work Barry and Suzy and their girls did to heal little Raun was even bigger. They worked day and night for over a year, reaching into little Raun's world, curing him of that dreaded disease. Bravo!

ALL DAY LONG the reviews keep coming in. *Son-Rise*, it seems, is a hit. America is deeply moved by the story. All except one man, a doctor, a well-known autism specialist.

"Mr. Rothman—you've done us a terrible disservice," he tells me on the phone.

"Really?" I'm surprised. "And how did I manage to do that?"

"False hope. You led people to believe you had a cure for autism."

"No, I didn't, Doctor. The film stated clearly from the beginning that we were *not* offering a cure—this was simply the story about how one family treated autism and cured their little boy. The story is true."

"The boy couldn't have been autistic!"

"Doctor, I have his records from nine of this country's finest clinics."

"Impossible! If he'd been autistic, he couldn't have been cured."

"Why do you say that?"

"Because autism is incurable!" he shouts.

"You mean *you've* never cured it, Doctor," I say, and hang up.

NOW WHY WOULD a highly credited doctor—and I'm sure a good one—say something like that? Even if the medical profession hadn't found a cure for the disease, why would he be so arrogant as to believe nobody could? Or ever will? I guess doctors are human like the rest of us—just as competitive, guarding their turf just as jealously.

Son-Rise was broadcast in 1978. It got giant ratings and super reviews, and it won a lot of prestigious awards. Autism was a little-known disease then. Today, sadly, it's much more widespread, far more frequently diagnosed. Happily, there have been a number of instances where a cure was reported. Someday autism will be wiped out. But it won't be an arrogant doctor who finds the cure.

27

SAY

G'NIGHT,

GRACIE

*T*HE CALL COMES IN EARLY ON A
Monday morning, when all calls are
serious. My partner, Jack, and I are still grunting over our
third cup of coffee when Molly comes in, annoyingly chip-
per, as is her usual early-morning demeanor. It isn't mine.

"It's Irving Fein," she informs us.

"That cheapskate!" says Jack.

I'd better explain. Irving Fein was George Burns's manager, had been Jack Benny's. He was a good manager—of the
old school—somewhat parsimonious. Make that very parsimonious. In fact, give it two or three *verys*. But that was part
of his job, after all, and I always felt he did it very well. You
see, George Burns and Jack Benny were best friends. As long
as Jack was alive, Irving felt he couldn't manage George—it
would be a conflict of interest. But now Jack had passed on,
and Irving was George's manager. His first act was to get
George a highly coveted acting job opposite Walter Matthau
in *The Sunshine Boys*. George was sensational in the picture.

"Irving's a good guy," I tell my partner.

"Yeah, I know, I know—he's just doing his job," says Jack.

So I pick up the phone. "CBS just gave George a special," Irving tells me in New Yorkese.

"Terrific," I say, "he deserves it."

"It's gonna be great! Listen who I booked for guest stars— I got Walter Matthau, Johnny Carson, Madeline Kahn— they're gonna be terrific!"

"Wow, what a lineup!" I say.

"The greatest," says Irving. "And wait'll you see the script!"

"Finished already?" I ask.

"I got George working on it with the writers next door. Gonna be great! Now all I need is to book my producers."

"What're you talking about, Irving?" I say, faking surprise. "You already got the show half-produced."

"More than half," he tells me. "But CBS wants accredited producers. I'm gonna exec-produce it."

"That's ridiculous," I tell him, 'cause I know where this is going. "You don't need producers."

"I know, I know, but the network wants what they want."

"So who do they want?" says I, knowing full well... heh, heh, heh!

Now he gets coy. "Jack always liked you. So does George. And anyway, like you said, the job's half-done..."

"Yeah, Irv, I don't think you need anyone."

"So what're you guys doing in January? I just need a month. Maybe six weeks."

"Yeah, I think we're open—we open in January, Jack?" I say to my partner, who has no idea what's going on. "We're fine in January, Irving."

"Good, good, 'cause I promised to get back to CBS today. Don't have a lot of dough for you guys—maybe seventy-five hundred dollars. But like I said, there's practically nothing for you to do."

"Go work it out with Sandy," I say, and hang up.

Now I call my agent, Sandy Wernick, to prepare him.

"Just got a call from Irving Fein," I tell him.

"That cheapskate?" he yells, not unexpectedly. "What's he want?"

"He wants us to produce *The George Burns Special* for CBS, that's what he wants."

"Fine," says Sandy. "What's he offering?"

"Not much," I say. "Seventy-five hundred."

"What?" he screams at me. "Are you crazy? It took me four and a half years to get your fee up to thirty-five thousand. You can't take that offer!"

"Sandy—George Burns is hot as a pistol. Every producer in town is after that show—there are some shows you do for the prestige. We gotta do it."

"Prestige, schmestige! Seventy-five hundred just isn't enough! Wait a minute—Irving's on the other line—I'm putting you on hold."

The next minute and a half are tense. Then Sandy gets back on the line. "That son-of-a-bitch!"

"What happened?"

"He offered five grand!"

SO IRVING FEIN, just doing his job, lets our agent work him back up to a $7,500 fee, and Jack and I are off and running the most sought-after special of the year.

I learn a lot from George Burns. Besides the fact that faking sincerity is the most important thing you can learn about acting. He also teaches us important things about how to tell a story.

"Lie!" he says. "It really helps. Fill in the extraneous details on the way to the story, and they'll believe it when you get to the punchline. True stories are funnier. I remember the time Gracie and I were arguing over dinner—I'll never forget it because she'd made the best pot roast I ever tasted—with carrots and onions and mushrooms—anyway, she was telling me about her best girlfriend, Rover, and I said, 'Rover? Your best girlfriend's name was Rover? Rover's a dog's name, Gracie.' 'That's what I always called her,' Gracie said. 'I remember the day her family moved in next door, and I said, "Mom—the family that moved in has a little girl my age, but I don't know her name." And my mom said, "Well, why don't you call her over?" So I did—I called her Rover'."

Now that story was pure fiction. All except the pot roast. That was real!

WE SHOOT THE show in front of a live audience in the Carol Burnett studio at CBS. We are shooting it in segments, so I build a little dressing room at the side of the stage where George can rest between segments. And I go back to prepare him for what's coming up next.

After the third or fourth segment, I notice something a little peculiar—each time I get back to talk to George, he has already taken off his tuxedo pants and is resting in his bathrobe.

"George," I say, "it's only a minute or two between scenes. Why are you changing in and out of your pants?"

"Well, kid, it's pretty easy," says George. "I grew up in vaudeville, where we did six shows a day. I only had one tuxedo. Couldn't afford to crease my pants!"

THE SHOW GOES smoothly and is very well received. The guest stars are especially enjoyable. We give Walter Matthau a big production number to sing in, not something he's used to doing. I think he must have forgotten his choreography, because he ends the number with his back to the audience, not the customary way to finish a production number. He looks so hilariously confused, completely out of step with the dancers, we decide to reshoot the ending, so as not to embarrass him.

"Why?" says Walter, "Wasn't it funny?"

"Well, sure, but..."

We take another look, and Walter is right—his ending is hilarious! Sometimes chaos is funny.

I WAS VERY impressed by Johnny Carson. He was certainly the most successful talk show host of his time, maybe of all time. But he shows up early for rehearsal, just sits quietly, watching, as George rehearses with the other guest stars. I thank him for coming on the show. "I should be thanking you for the privilege," he says modestly. "I grew up watching George Burns and Jack Benny. They taught me everything I know about comedy. Those guys invented timing."

A true gentleman.

GEORGE IS AMAZING. Years later, we run into each other—I don't think he remembers my name—but he recognizes me. He's just finished a picture. "How'd it go?" I ask him.

"Great," he says. "Best thing I've ever done."

He's eighty-seven years old. Doesn't matter whether it's really his best work. He thinks it is. Amazing!

28

TWO

BIRDS ON

A WIRE

∨

*T*HIS IS A VALENTINE FOR MY FRIEND
Leonard Cohen.

Cohen and I have been friends since we were eleven years old. "'Scuse me, Rothman," I can hear him saying, "you were eleven, I was ten." True enough, I was a year older but just as immature. And we were still in grade school, which is why we call each other by our last names, just like we did when we were eleven (sorry, Cohen, eleven and ten, respectively). To trace his career would take an encyclopedia-length book of its own. And I'm no Cohen maven, so I won't bother. What you'll get from me is a few personal notes, and I hope he won't mind.

I don't know anyone who uses the English language more beautifully. No poet captures the human spirit or describes the psychic landscape better than Cohen. No one's writing has ever warmed my romantic heart like Cohen's has. Not Shelley's, not Byron's, not Tennyson's—no one's.

We met at summer camp in northern Ontario, where we discovered girls together. Although Cohen already knew everything important to know about them. And what we really discovered was how much we liked them. Still do.

Cohen lived ten minutes away from me in Montreal. He still lives ten minutes away from me. In Los Angeles. Once a month we try to have lunch at the swanky Beverly Wilshire Hotel. There's Cohen, in his dark silk finery, Rothman in his McGill blazer, and—surprise!—we talk about women. For four hours. And giggle like the teenagers we still are. When we run out of girl talk, and it's time to go, Cohen says, "They'll never get us, Rothman." And I echo: "They'll never take us alive." Serious business.

We were romantics from an early age, began writing poems in puberty. There was always a girl to inspire us. My first real crush was Dundi, a cute Hungarian trollop, who dumped me, saying I was much too young (twelve) for her. In those days, having a girlfriend who was two years older was an insurmountable problem. I moped for months. Cohen's first heartthrob (and there were many) was the French maid (hardly a goddess), for whom Cohen turned his lecherous aspirations into Byronic odes. Cohen's poetry was brilliant, beautiful, right from the beginning. And to this day, there's not a single line he writes that doesn't stir my soul.

COHEN LEARNED TO play guitar in his teens. It was the age of hootenannies, and he entertained us all, singing the songs of famous folk artists of the day. He was a born entertainer—doesn't have a pretty voice, but he sings a great story, tells a great song. We listened in his living room, at the frat house, his flat on Stanley Street, his hotel room in New York. He didn't just spellbind us, he reached inside us, no matter whose material he was performing. He sang a prison song I'd written for a college show and made it sound like a Woody Guthrie classic.

I don't know when he started to perform professionally; I suspect it was in the late '50s. I first saw him at UCLA. It's the late '60s, and student rebellion is in bloom. Royce Hall is jammed, mostly with students, all excited to be there. In the middle of his performance, a young guy strides on stage and sits down beside Leonard. There's something strange about him—a look in his eye—he's surly, and the hall tenses up.

Cohen finishes his song and turns to the guy: "Something I can do for you?" he says calmly.

"No," comes the angry reply. "I got a right to be up here too." Scary.

Then Cohen says, "Absolutely. Everyone has a right to be up here. Why don't you all come up and join me on stage," he says to the audience. And they do. Weirdo defused. Great concert, happy audience.

LEONARD COHEN IS a very funny man. His audiences don't see that side of him. He's the prophet of the soul, an icon of the heart, and they refuse to see the lighter side of him. Maybe he shouldn't wear black. But even in concert, when he plucks out two bars on the piano in the middle of an orchestral interlude—does it with one finger—the audience applauds—and Cohen says, straight-faced, "Thank you, music lovers." Some get it, some don't.

But throughout the many years of our friendship, there's been a determination to remain silly.

We're in New York. I'm writing a Bell Telephone special, Cohen is working with his editor on *Beautiful Losers,* and we meet for a late supper. We must've been a bit high on something (either the work or the wine), because we're dancing down the streets like a couple of fools at two o'clock in the morning. Suddenly, Cohen sees something and stops. A sign outside the restaurant: The Stork Club. Inside, it's dark and deserted. "I finally figured out what they do in there, Rothman," says Cohen.

"What?"

"They club storks."

Cohen always loved Montreal, kept a home there and wherever else he lived—Greece, Nashville, New York, Los Angeles—he's lived around the world for more than forty years. So have I. Toronto, New York, London, Los Angeles, Sydney—we both followed wherever our hearts would lead us. Last month I received the following e-mail:

> dear old rothman
> writing from montreal
> come home
> we made a big mistake
> old cohen

After forty years?

ANOTHER OF COHEN'S lesser known characteristics is his graciousness. He has the best manners I've ever experienced. Nothing phony; he's just a very kind, very thoughtful person. I forwarded him one of those borderline-maudlin e-mails someone sent me about friendship, with an accompanying note that said, "After fifty-seven years I guess we can call each other friends." And he wrote back, "Fifty-seven years is just the beginning, old rothman."

Never had a better friend.

29

"GET A

JOB" — '50S

STYLE

So NOW YOU KNOW—THIS BOOK—
this nonmemoir or whatever we're
gonna call it—is not about me. It's about a lot of famous
people I worked with over the years as a TV writer and producer. They were all interesting. Most of them were very talented. Some of them, brilliant. A few were geniuses. Then
there was Sha Na Na.

Sha Na Na made their flashy concert debut as a novelty
'50s rock act at the Woodstock Festival, then rapidly disappeared. Now, in the mid-1970s, impresario Pierre Cossette
sells a sponsor on the idea of building a show around them.
Kind of a musical *Happy Days* (sounds good, but what does
it mean?). Pierre hires my partner and me to create and produce the show. We fly to New York to see them perform.

Twenty thousand screaming fans at Madison Square
Gardens—half a dozen boisterous rock groups singing their
hits, and then Sha Na Na, singing everyone else's. They're
the loudest, sloppiest, most out of tune of them all, and the
audience loves them. Trouble is, there's no act, or none that

we can make a series out of. Ten guys in a group singing a bunch of other groups' hits. Okay for a one-shot special, but not a series. They'll run out of material by the middle of the first year. And who's our leader, the one guy an audience can identify with? Bowzer? Maybe. But every one of these greasers thinks he's the star. Chaos!

Next morning over brunch in his hotel suite, a smiling Pierre Cossette pops the question—the question Jack and I had lost sleep over because we knew he'd ask it. "Well guys," the cheery impresario says, "what are we going to do with Sha Na Na?"

Jack and I look at each other. I gulp and go first. "Give your sponsor his money back," I tell him.

Pierre blanches.

Jack went on. "With all the talented performers around, people are gonna wonder how come these losers got their own series."

Pierre is devastated. But that's part of the strategy. Our show concept is so radical we're sure he'll turn us down if we just pitch it. Now we've got him worried enough he may just buy it.

"Pierre, these guys made their names singing like a street gang," Jack says. "Kids love it. But we don't think grown-ups will."

Pierre is looking very depressed.

"So we put 'em in a Brooklyn street scene, dress 'em like the greasers they are, and let 'em sing. When they finish, instead of ovations, we throw insults at them."

"Are you guys nuts?" says Pierre.

"Probably," I say. "But it's going to work. Audiences eat that stuff up. Most stand-up comics make a living on insult comedy. We'll create neighbors for the boys, characters who live on the street. When our boys finish a number, a lady opens her window and yells down, 'Hey, will you cut out that racket—I'm tryin' to sleep!' A street cop suggests 'Why don't ya try something else next time—maybe music.'"

Pierre is laughing, but still a bit dubious. "Why can't you just let 'em sing?"

"Because people will compare them to every other rock group. And honestly, Pierre—you really think they sing as well as the Mamas and the Papas?"

Jack adds: "This way, we'll get big laughs for the insults, and audiences will say, 'Hey, they're not that bad.'"

Well, it works. The series is promoted as "the only show on television that leaves a ring around your set." Jack and I produce the pilot and the first year's episodes. We hire a super staff to work with the boys, and the writers, with director Walter Miller, keep those insults coming. The show's an instant hit and runs for four season.

I'm not sure Sha Na Na ever forgave us for all those insults, but I think we did them a favor. And you know what—they turned out to be pretty good entertainers after all.

30

THE SUITS

*I*S THERE ANYONE WHO DOESN'T know who the Suits are? Who maybe thinks I'm referring to a rack of clothes in a tailor shop? No takers? I thought not.

"The Suits," in showbiz parlance, is a pejorative for executives in the entertainment industry. Network executives, studio types, agents—you know, the guys and gals who have to wear suits to work. Like your banker. The inference is that they've got no more creative talent than your banker. So why don't they just shut up and write you a check, like your banker? Usually, they're the buyers, so they wield enormous power—life and death—over your work.

Naturally, you like the ones who buy from you, look down on the cretins who don't. Obviously, the "don't-buyers" have no taste. Whereas the buyers are brilliant—geniuses with infallible taste and judgment. Until they dare to interfere with your lofty creative endeavors by making an occasional suggestion. Then they're dispatched from the genius class to the cretins!

Okay, here's how it works. You got an idea for a series? Go see the development VP of drama, comedy, sports, whatever, at one of the networks. Pitch the idea (tell it, don't sell it) as fully as possible—the characters, the types of stories, the style, and so on. If he likes it, he'll ask for a brief outline of a pilot episode—it should be typical of ensuing episodes in the series. He may tell you he's got something like it in development, which means you're on the right track. So go home and bring him another idea—a slightly different one—next week. This time he tells you it's too similar to something else he's got. He wants something completely different, off the beaten track, like... Now he proceeds to describe something you saw on the opposing network last Wednesday.

Try again. Third time lucky. Loves this one, wants to put it in development. The two of you hammer out an outline for a pilot script, and off you go with his order to have your agent call the network's VP, Business Affairs. (No one who works for a network isn't a VP.)

It takes a while, but the deal is made. You're surprised at how much they're going to pay you. But you'll work for your money. You're expected to deliver a polished script, along with a "bible," which is a breakdown of characters, their backgrounds, and how they interact in a variety of story lines.

Delivery deadline is four to six weeks. In five weeks, you deliver a script you're thrilled with. You wait patiently to hear back, confident they'll love it. A week later you're called in for "notes." "Notes" is a session in which the network dudes get to criticize, complain, ruin your work, and generally throw their weight around—know what I mean? "That's not the show we bought," our development

VP whines. That's the first thing they all say. I fought it for years. What're they talking about? I followed our outline carefully, studied my notes from the meeting—it was *exactly* what I sold them.

Then I figure it out. It may have been what I sold, but it wasn't what they bought! They had a completely different idea of what the show was about. No point arguing. Figure out what their vision is, *and give it to them*. They're the buyers, for chrissake! And no matter how stupid their idea is, make it work. 'Cause if it doesn't, it's your fault—you screwed up his idea! You can't win with a Suit. Best you can get is a draw.

TRUTHFULLY, NOT ALL Suits are idiots. 'Zmatter of fact, most of the network types I worked with were bright, talented, and very knowledgeable. (Which didn't stop me from hating them when they turned me down.) Some of them actually had integrity, would go to bat with their bosses if they believed you were right. Marcy Carsey, for instance, in her days as ABC's comedy maven—she'd fight you tooth and nail over a minor character or a plot point. In the end she'd say, "Know what? It's your show. You created it, and you know it best. Let's do it your way." Then she'd go to her boss and fight to get your show on the air. Strong personality, and smart. No wonder she and her partner became so incredibly successful when they formed their own production company.

Michael Ogiens was another of the great ones. No nonsense. You'd pitch an idea, and in the middle of your first paragraph, he'd say, "Naw, I don't wanna do that."

"Well, why, Mike?"

"I don't like it, that's all."

End of debate. Next week, just as quickly he'd say, "Hey, I like that." And go next door into Bud Grant's office (CBS president at the time), put his job on the line, and get us a production commitment. Once when we told him we'd lost money on one of his shows, he got us a rerun on another. Got us paid enough for the rerun to more than make up the difference. That kind of Suit you'd work your buns off for. And he'd roll up his sleeves, get down there in the trenches, and work with you. So you wouldn't mind so much when, once in a while, he'd say, "Naw, I don't wanna do that," to one of your ideas. Even if he said it before you got the first words out of your mouth. Michael Ogiens had a great string of network hits because he knew what he was doing and wasn't afraid to take a chance. He'd take a chance on you, too, if he thought you knew what you were doing. Terrific man!

ANDY SIEGEL WAS another creative network vice president whom we liked working with. Andy was head of comedy development at ABC when we met. His father, the late Sol Siegel, had been a big-time Hollywood film producer, but Andy had none of his dad's strut. He liked writing and writers, wrote well, and related well to creative people.

We come to Andy with a project my ex-partner, Stan Jacobson, brought to us that is kind of interesting. It's an adaptation of the long-running Canadian series *The Plouffe Family,* about a French-Canadian family living in an English neighborhood in Montreal. Stan's version centers on a Latino family living in the barrio in Los Angeles. We call it *Viva Valdez.*

To our shock, Andy buys the project, gives us development money, and lo, for the first time, Jack and I are in the sitcom business. We have no track record as comedy pilot writers (I had written some comedy episodes of *My Three*

Sons, but neither Jack nor Stan had ever written for the medium), so we have to hire sitcom specialists to do the job. Being the show's producers, we would supervise the writers, but alas, no money unless the script sells. Another surprise—the script sells. So we're green-lighted to produce the pilot for our first comedy venture. Bravo! I'm really looking forward to the experience. Unfortunately, I'll have to be in New York producing "Danny Kaye at the Met," while the *Viva Valdez* pilot is being shot in L.A. My partners will have to do the job. We have strict deadlines, and that really pisses me off!

But as that other great sitcom writer, Ernest Hemingway, once said, "A man must do what he must do," which means more jokes on page 7. So I spend a month in the Big Apple (one of my least favorite cities in the world) producing a monster musical special, worried out of my mind that Jack and Stan will screw up on the sitcom pilot and we'll never get another chance.

Two more surprises: without Jack's help, I win us our first Emmy Award for "Danny Kaye at the Met." And Jack and Stan get our series—no, our very first network situation comedy series—picked up on the basis of the pilot they produced, with absolutely no help from me! Now that *really* pisses me off!

So *Viva Valdez* is launched—the first Latino series on a major network. Respectable numbers (maybe 25 percent of the sets in use watch it—good numbers for today—not in those days), but not good enough to stay on the air past our initial order of thirteen episodes.

So now Jack and I are sitcom producers. Another surprise. Our friend Andy Siegel leaves ABC for the comedy job at CBS. And Andy invites us to come pitch shows to him at his new home. Heaven!

We visit Andy's new quarters once, twice, three times, four times, each time pitching two new shows. And each time he turns us down, with fresh, albeit legitimate, reasons. That's eight turndowns! And each show we pitch takes a week to develop—characters, story lines—the works. So we're very discouraged. But Andy won't let go.

"I really like your stuff," he tells us each time. Jack and I are rolling our eyes by now. "Ya gotta trust me. We'll find the right fit, guys." And on the fifth try, we do. In fact, Andy buys two shows from us that day. Rolls up his sleeves and helps us develop them. One of them goes to pilot. And they let us write the scripts. Which they pay good money for. And even though we're never hugely successful in that market, Jack and I become part of the chosen few who are allowed to write pilot scripts. Which we do—two or three a year—for CBS, for ABC—for the next seven years. Nice. Keeps us feeding our families for quite some time.

31

LES GIRLS

*A*FTER THE WORLD OF SITCOMS, THE Kathy Miller story in 1978 was quite a switch for me. In real life, Kathy was a pretty girl in her midteens who was run down by a truck, smashing most of the bones in her body. She fell into a deep, long-term coma, and her doctors gave the family little hope for the girl's survival. But Kathy's mother wouldn't forsake her daughter, spent hours every day talking to her, hoping that one day her beloved little girl would answer back.

The first thing our director, Bob Lewis, does right— maybe the best thing—is refuse to accept anyone playing the title role who is less than an excellent actress. We spend months in the casting studio, auditioning dozens of attractive, highly competent young actresses. Finally, there is one I kind of like.

"Yes, she's good," says Bob. "But good isn't good enough. Bernie, we need a fabulous actress for this role. She's got to carry it. She *is* the movie."

"You're the director," I tell him. "Direct her. She's good now; you'll make her great."

"Bernie, it doesn't happen that way. With a short rehearsal schedule, what you see is what you get."

"Then what do we do? We've seen every actress in town." I am discouraged.

"That's not true," he reminds me. "We've only seen actresses who are seventeen and older. Maybe we'll find a sixteen-year-old..."

Milt Hammerman, our casting director, interrupts: "If she's under seventeen, you can only work her half-days, Bob."

"Better half a day with someone good than a whole day with someone half-good."

My partner agrees: "He's right, Milt. Who ya got?"

Milt is already thumbing through his files. He stops, pulls out an 8 x 10 glossy. She's young and attractive, certainly not as glamorous as some of the girls we've seen.

Milt is unsure: "She just turned sixteen. Her father's an acting coach, so she's been acting since she was a kid. Never played anything this big, but..."

"Bring her in," we all say in unison.

"Tomorrow," says Milt. "If she's available."

She's available. And that's how we meet sixteen-year-old Helen Hunt.

HELEN IS FABULOUS from her first reading. She has a cute sense of humor, and if she's nervous, she sure covers it beautifully. Moreover, she's so real, so convincing in the role, she easily holds her own with the two more experienced leads—Sharon Gless and Frank Converse. Helen and Sharon get along like two kids on a playground. They're both fun, funny, smart, and talented. When Helen needs a little bolstering—which is rare—Sharon is there to big-sister her, help her interpret the role. When Sharon gets too intense,

Helen clowns to loosen her up—makes faces, cracks wise. And of course, they spend a lot of time talking about boys. They are a great team.

The movie turns out very well. Helen gives a virtuoso performance. And the chemistry between the two women is magic. We watch, fascinated, as the mother lovingly talks her lifeless daughter out of the coma. Slowly, painfully, the girl begins to recover. We can feel the creaking in young Kathy Miller's broken limbs as they mend, little by little, day by day, gaining strength. Until once again she becomes the person she was before her dreadful accident. Challenging job for a young actress, especially since we shoot the scenes out of sequence. Then the race—Kathy, still on the mend, enters a marathon. (She was a long-distance runner before her accident.) She doesn't expect to win, but she's determined to finish. Helen Hunt is not much of an athlete. But she runs Kathy's race for her, and her struggle is riveting.

They're all good, of course—the whole cast. And Bob shoots the film beautifully. On set, the girls are hilarious every day. They sing, they laugh, they cavort. At least until the cameras roll. Then they get serious. Very.

We're nominated for the Governor's Media Award. We don't win it, but it's nice to be nominated, isn't it?

Watching Helen Hunt's career since that time has delighted me. And her performance opposite Jack Nicholson in *As Good As It Gets* was as good as it gets!

Helen was wonderful at sixteen, and every year she gets wonderful-er.

MY SISTER SAM was another tough one to cast.

It's a sitcom pilot my friend Burt Metcalfe and I are producing for Warner Brothers Television and CBS. It centers on Pam Dawber, who plays Samantha, a new-age, independent-minded young woman who's come from a small Midwestern town in search of a commercial artist's career in the big city. Simple, uncomplicated, and doing fine, until her fifteen-year-old kid sister decides to leave home and move in with her. The problem for Sam is the sudden role of mothering her kid sister while acclimatizing herself to the vicissitudes of big-city life. The problem for Burt and me is finding a teen-age actress with enough talent and experience to hold her own in a costarring role with Pam. Not easy. Who would be Sam's sister?

Again, after weeks of casting sessions, seeing lots of *nearly*-good-enough young actresses, we're discouraged. The rest of the cast is set. It's Friday; we're due to begin rehearsals on Monday. Still no sister for Sam.

Then we hear about a young actress named Rebecca Schaeffer who played a featured role in a not-yet-released Woody Allen movie. Since Woody is renowned for his actress discoveries, we decide to put off rehearsals a day or two and fly the young lady in from her home in Oregon for an audition.

Rebecca is great at her audition, plays Sam's sister perfectly. Her chemistry with Pam Dawber, a very unselfish actress, is immediate. That's what gets the series on the air. They really *are* sisters. They talk like sisters, argue like sisters, laugh like sisters, fight like sisters, make up like sisters, reminisce like sisters—they're amazing. Pam Dawber has never been better, and America discovers a new young star. Rebecca is brilliant! Sounds like a happy ending, doesn't it? It isn't. Not happy at all.

In the show's second season, a stalker takes a liking to the radiant Miss Schaeffer, follows her home, and murders her.

I had plenty of sleepless nights over this tragedy. I still feel guilty. The show was a struggle from the beginning. We argued with Warners over everything—every move they made. We never trusted them, and, I suspect, the feeling was mutual. Our only enjoyment was working with Pam and Rebecca. But the pilot we produced was good enough for CBS to go forward with. We didn't have to stay with the series, because, happily, Warner Brothers bought out our contracts. Little did we know that God would buy out Rebecca's.

Burt and I got paid a lot of money for producing that pilot. It wasn't worth it. I swear to you, if refunding every nickel would buy back the time, or, miraculously, bring back Rebecca, we'd happily do it. In a Montreal minute.

Rebecca Schaeffer was a wonderful young woman, heading, at warp speed, for superstardom. She did nothing but spread joy and sunshine into every corner of the room. We all miss her.

Helen Hunt, grâce à Dieu, still lives on this planet. I wish her many happy years to come. Life is ephemeral.

32

A WEEKEND

WITH CONNIE

AND MAURY

*T*HEY WERE DEFINITELY THE MOST charming couple in Hollywood. Then they moved to New York, where they were just as charming. Maybe charming-er. And just as smart and lively and well informed and, well—adorable. But they were funnier in Hollywood than in New York. Especially Maury. He could be funny in a golf shirt, but not in his Brooks Brothers suit. And his wing tips got in the way of his funniness. Connie could be funny with anything. Except Dan Rather, with whom she co-anchored in New York for a year or two. Good man, Dan Rather, but nobody's funny around him. No offense, Dan.

It's 1977, Connie Chung and Maury Povich are both anchors on the local evening news. Only at different networks. Maybe that's what took them so long to get married—their networks kept sending them to different cities. But they're both anchoring for CBS in L.A. when we meet them. They start dating in 1978, after Maury gets shipped off to San Francisco, which makes dating a little awkward. But they sure are in love.

Interesting backgrounds, these two—Connie's dad worked for the Chinese Embassy in Washington. She is the youngest of five sisters, in a close-knit family, and she acts like it. Maury is the son of a famous Washington sports columnist. He's the family prince, and a "scratch" golfer. But he doesn't act like one. Not Maury. 'Cept on the golf course. They're both real cool dudes.

Connie and Maury are good friends of our friends Peter and Laurie Grad. The two young men went to college together—U of Penn—picked up the relationship when the Grads moved to California, where Peter went to work for Paramount Pictures. This was 1978, and by then, Connie and Maury had begun dating. The two couples became fast friends. Inseparable.

Alas, the inseparables got separated. Maury was moved to a co-anchorship at station KGO, San Francisco. Connie stayed on in L.A. anchoring the evening news, remained friendly with the Grads, and the two couples spent time together whenever Maury came to town. Which was often, because he dearly loved lovable Connie, whom we fell in love with first time we met. We fell in love with Maury too, an absolutely terrific man. We hoped he and Connie would get married, and of course, a few years later, they did.

I also fell in love with Connie's little English sports car, a Jensen Healey. I wanted to buy it from her if she ever decided to get rid of it, which she did, and I did, when she moved to New York to do the NBC national news. But hey—am I getting ahead of myself?

From time to time we'd have dinner with them when Maury was in town, and it was always great fun. The greatest, funnest of all—a weekend in San Francisco, celebrating Maury's fortieth birthday. There were forty of us. And we knew Maury didn't want to be forty. And he didn't want to be away from Connie while he was getting there. We also knew he wasn't very flush at the time. But what with all this going against him, he was determined to celebrate in grand style, 'cause, y'see, friends mean a great deal to Maury, and he wanted his friends around him when he turned that awful number. So, celebrate we did—on a beautiful summer weekend in San Francisco.

We got up there late Friday afternoon. By seven, we were out with the Grads for dinner at one of those old-fashioned French joints on Nob Hill, 'cause in those days they had a million fancy French joints, and we had none in Los Angeles. None that were any good. After dinner was even better. See, Maury knew all about San Francisco. He'd been living there for practically a whole year, hobnobbed with the hoi polloi, knew every boîte in town. So he swept Connie off to a secret Friday night dinner, and arranged to meet us at quite possibly the most elegant cocktail bar I've ever been to in my whole life. Le Trianon. Gorgeous!

Crystal chandeliers, potted palms, red velvet swags, and an enormous ebony grand piano, spotlighted right in the middle of the room.

I must've had four whiskey sours before my wife stopped me. Not because I was drunk—although I *was* drunk. But a rather striking-looking young man had entered the room, to a smattering of polite applause from the sophisticated carriage-trade audience, and sat down at the piano. He was dressed in white tie and tails, his long blond hair parted smack in the middle of his head. Couldn't have been more than twenty-seven—if that—but his style of piano playing belied his years. He swept aside his tails and began playing: Cole Porter, George Gershwin, Irving Berlin, Rodgers and Hart, Jerome Kern—the whole brittle bunch of 'em. Amazing that he knew all these tunes—they were written years before this kid was born. What was more astonishing was how he played them—exactly like cocktail pianists had played them thirty years before. I know, 'cause I was around then. Every nuance was there, every '30s and '40s lick. Bobbi and I loved it. So did everybody else. Peter Minton was the boy-genius piano player. We stayed all night. Would've stayed longer if they hadn't closed the bar.

I don't remember what I did Saturday afternoon. But I remember what Bobbi did. She went shopping with Connie and Laurie. (Shopping is what women do instead of playing golf.) At Wilkes Bashford. Gorgeous stuff, costs a fortune. Knowing how important clothes are to Connie in her professional life, Bobbi wonders how she can afford all this stuff.

"Not easy," says Connie. "But I just buy the tops!"

Of course. I never stopped to figure it out—the rest of her is hidden by that neat little anchor desk—no bottoms necessary! Well, nothing fancy, anyway.

And then the party. Whatta party! In the dark-and-dusty candlelit wine cellar of an old Italian restaurant in North Beach. I don't remember what we ate—it was good, of course—traditional Neapolitan fare, none of this risotto or polenta—no siree. Just meat dishes—veal and chicken—accompanied by pastas, mostly covered in red sauce, like the real Italian food we grew up with. Delicious. And for dessert, it seems tiramisu hadn't yet been invented, so we had something better—fresh fruit with a vintage Parmigiano Reggiano cheese. And a great sweet Italian dessert wine to drink with it. Mmmm!

There are forty people at the party, happy people who love Connie and Maury. Old friends who flew in from L.A. and New York and Washington and Philadelphia and

Chicago—cities where Maury had lived and worked. Plus a bunch of new friends Maury had made in San Francisco. (He makes friends easily—like I said, the man is charming.)

We're all happy to be included, happy to be celebrating, happy to hang out with Connie and Maury, two of everybody's favorite people. And when it's all over, the restaurant owner, a delightful old Italian-American named Lorenzo Patrone (can you get any more Italian than that?), gives the party a happy ending by picking up most of the tab. Happy birthday, Maury Povich!

ANOTHER TIME WE have a Chinese cook-off. With Laurie, Connie, and me doing the cooking and our spouses doing the enjoying. We have it at our house in Beverly Hills, and the idea is we'd each prepare two Chinese dishes and then finish them, last minute, on my stove. 'Cause you know, Chinese food has to be eaten hot-off-the-stove to taste right.

Six dishes. I make Mongolian Beef and Szechuan Eggplant, Laurie makes Kung Pao Scallops and Tangerine Chicken, and Connie makes Lo Mein Noodles and shrimp balls. Quite a feast. They're all good dishes, but—no contest—Connie's shrimp dish is by far the best—miles ahead of the rest.

"Of course it's the best," says Peter Grad, "but she cheated—she's Chinese!"

None of us had any idea Connie was such a fabulous cook.

"How'd you make it?" we all want to know. "C'mon, Connie, give us your recipe! Share your secrets with us!"

Connie resists, but we persist: "All right, all right already!" says the little Orienta-yenta. "I'll tell you how it's done. But it's a secret recipe—not everyone can make it this way." And she starts:

"First of all, you gotta get up very early in the morning..."

"Yes, yes," Laurie says. "Get on with it."

Connie continues: "Then you call to your mother in Van Nuys..."

"My mother's in New York," interrupts Bobbi.

Connie continues, unfazed: "Like I said—not everyone can make this recipe. When your mother answers, you say, 'Mom—do me a favor—make up a big batch of that shrimp batter from Grandma's recipe and I'll come over and pick it up this afternoon.' That's the way it's done. You just drop spoonfuls of my mother's batter in hot oil and fry 'em till the shrimp balls are nicely browned. Simple, eh? And, by the way, my mother will be delighted to hear from you. Surprised but delighted."

WHEN CONNIE MOVES to New York to do NBC national newscasts, she sells me her great little Jensen Healey. For practically free.

"I know you'll give it a good home," she tells me.

And I do. And when my son Mike comes back from Hawaii, I give it to him. He gives it a good home, too. But it gets to be too small for his wife and kids. So I call Connie and she takes our baby back. I wonder if that car ever knew it was adopted.

I MISS CONNIE and Maury. Very much. They're two of the warmest, kindest, classiest people I know. Very, very talented. I'm thrilled for them, for all the good things that have happened. Lots has: Connie's rise to nationwide fame, Maury's immensely successful series, and that beloved ten-year-old boy they adore, who's lucky enough to have them as parents.

Television people are like gypsies. You're thrown together by happenstance, and before you know it, you've got to follow your career to another city. Or country. And some of the friends you leave behind you wish you didn't have to. But the good ones leave you with memories. And those you keep forever.

33

WINTER

CARNIVAL

*T*ORONTO. FRIDAY AFTERNOON, A week before Christmas, 1986. I'm in Toronto prepping for the Genie Awards, Canada's equivalent to the Oscars, also given in early spring. I'm shutting down my office, going back to my hotel. By Sunday afternoon I'll be back in L.A.

Ring, ring, ring. A woman's voice, mildly flavored with French Canada. Do I know of a Monsieur Marcel Aubut, she asks me. Indeed, I do—he's the famous owner of the Quebec Nordiques hockey team, I tell her, without revealing that the information came to me only that day from Garry Blye, my production-oriented line producer, who knows everyone and everything. Well, it appears Monsieur Aubut has something important to talk to me about—would I mind holding on the line? Well, I wouldn't and I do and we talk. Here's the story:

It's the Nordiques' turn to hold the all-star NHL game on their home ice. Marcel Aubut feels that annual event is boring, so he invites the Russians to form their own all-star team and come play the NHL's best. It takes a few months, but the Russkies accept. Now remember, this is 1986—a couple of years before glasnost. This is a very big deal! So Marcel decides to make a big thing of it—stage the whole thing during Quebec's Winter Carnival week, invite the Americans and the Russians to participate in fashion shows, ice sculpting, all kinds of sporting competition—the works. The week of events, to be known as Rendezvous '87, will end with great entertainers from all three countries performing in a spectacular gala at Quebec's Grand Theatre. Would I be interested in producing said gala? Would I? Ha!

Next morning, I'm on Marcel's private plane on the way to Quebec City. He's promised me I'll be back by nightfall. Marcel is a large man—over six feet, easily 230 pounds. When he tells me about his project, there's a passion I can't resist. He's already booked Alan Thicke to be the host and write the script, he's got David Foster to do the music, and he's lined up a luscious bevy of guest stars awaiting my approval—Ben Vereen, Crystal Gayle, Paul Anka, Louis Anderson, the Bolshoi Ballet, the Red Army Chorus—all the greats and near-greats. Wow!

I'm very excited and agree to do the show. Now take me home, Marcel. Sure. But first we have to make the deal. I give him my agent's number, but that's not enough. He wants a deal. Now! We talk terms for an hour, and he sends me out for lunch. A delicious lunch with a delicious lady who owns a delicious restaurant all decorated for Christmas. After lunch, Marcel and I sign the contract, and then he gives me the bad news—the large plane I flew up in is no longer available. I go back in a three-seater, flown by two pilots who look like they're still in their teens. I'm shaking as we fly through a blizzard, but we make it. To the wrong airport.

Then a limousine to the right one. Then back to the hotel and back to L.A. Whew!

WHEN I RETURN, Quebec is a fairyland, its ancient gray buildings all covered in white, glistening with ice sculptures on every street. The town's alive with a joyous winter carnival. The streets are full; so are the pubs. Everyone's celebrating!

I don't love Alan Thicke's script. Too flip. Should be classier, reflect the importance of the occasion. Alan agrees. So I bring in Mark Shekter, and together we rewrite it. "Togetherness" ideas, reflecting the two cultures—East and West. First idea—get Alan Thicke together with three guys from the Red Army Chorus, form a barbershop quartet, and have them sing a couple of verses of "Sweet Adeline." Takes us two months to negotiate; we finally close the deal on the day of the show. On stage, Alan and his barbershop gang are hilarious. The audience screams for an encore. Pity! Our quartet only knows "Sweet Adeline."

Backstage, it's a traffic jam. There are at least 150 in the cast, including singers, dancers, musicians, a Russian rock group, a 40-member dance ensemble, a huge male chorus, and the entire RCMP marching band. Plus 85 guys the KGB sent over in case anybody gets out of line.

The show is a powerful one; the audience is spellbound. Director Stan Harris's vision—waves of Russian soldiers marching over the hill, filling the hall with their mighty baritone war songs—awesome! Then the plea for peace—"Shenandoah." The mighty Russians singing our sweet folk song—beautiful! The lovely Russian dancing girls with their acrobatic Kazatzke partners. Crystal Gayle, her flowing brown hair dancing to her mellow Nashville sounds. Hit after hit. And Louis Anderson—all three hundred pounds of him. "I can't stay long," he says, grinning, "I'm between meals." Audience eats him up!

I really like Alan Thicke's improvised closing curtain speech. He tells the truth—that we all feel we've been party to a very special event, and it's brought us all together. That in years to come, we'll think of Rendezvous '87 as a turning point.

Hockey? They play two matches. The Russians win the first; the NHL wins the second. Best hockey, ever!

It didn't take long for the wall to come down.

BUT THERE WAS never a wall between Anthony Newley and me. I loved the man. Tony had more natural high-class class than anyone this side of the Royals. Not bad for a cockney kid, born on the wrong side of the tracks in a country that looks down on its impoverished. Tony somehow picked himself up, taught himself music and acting, started right at the bottom as a child actor, and rose to superstardom on Broadway and in Hollywood. And for those of you saying, "Big deal! Cary Grant did it before him and made it even bigger," Cary couldn't sing and didn't star in hit musicals that he wrote. I'm talking about *The Roar of the Greasepaint* and *Stop the World, I Want to Get Off,* among others, full of amazing hit songs. And a number of stellar appearances he made on stage, on television, in films.

Tony and I become friends because we live near each other. He guest-stars in a couple of TV specials that I produce in the late '70s—not my best work, but Tony is always terrific. He's a perfectionist, stays on to rehearse long after the rest of the cast has gone home. It has to be right.

Tony plays as hard as he works. He was married to glamorous actress Joan Collins, and for years they were the darlings of London society. I remember having lunch with him and my friend Burt Metcalfe (*M*A*S*H*'s producer), who asks him what was the most memorable thing about his marriage to Joan. "The parties!" he says with palpable relish. "Joan threw the most fabulous parties!" End of her good points. The marriage ended badly, sorry to say, and his ex said some nasty things about Tony in her book. I never heard him say anything nice about her after the book came out. A gentleman need only be a gentleman up to a point.

TONY CALLS ONE day to say he is going to Toronto to make a film, taking the family with him, would be there for several months. Any advice? I give him Renee's phone number. "She's a great woman, Tony. Call her for anything you need." I love my sister.

Well, they need a pediatrician while they're there, and Tony figures my sister would know a good one. So he phones her.

Ring, ring, ring. "Hello..."

"Mrs. Simmons?"

Cautiously, "Yes..."

"Mrs. Simmons, this is Anthony Newley."

"Sure it is," says Renee, "and I'm the Queen of Romania."

She hangs up. Newley tries again.

Ring, ring, ring.

"Hello..."

"Mrs. Simmons, this really is Anthony Newley, I'm a friend of your brother's."

"Sure you are, and so's Rich Little, and he does a helluva lot better impression of Tony Newley than you do." Another hang-up. Now Tony calls me out of complete frustration. I apologize for not telling Renee to expect his call. "Call her again in ten minutes," I say. "I'll fix it up."

Now I call my sister and work out a plan that'll really make Tony crazy.

Ring, ring, ring. A male voice: "Hello..."

"Is Mrs. Simmons there please?"

"No, she's gone out. This is Mr. Simmons. Who's speaking?"

"This is Anthony Newley."

"Oh," says my brother-in-law, "so you're sticking to the same old story, are you?"

Tony is just starting to get abusive when my sister gets on the phone and confesses: it was all a ruse. And by that time, Newley tells my sister he no longer needs a pediatrician—does she know a good shrink?

LAST I SEE Tony Newley is up at our little market atop Beverly Glen. He's with his young son, Sasha, on a visit from England. He's been ill, had gone home to spend his remaining days. Cancer had once again afflicted him, and he wanted to spare his young family the grief of his suffering. We talk about the good times we'd spent together and a project we'd both loved but never finished: *Live, from Planet Earth* it was called.

"Think you can sell it?" he asks.

"Maybe. But I don't have a copy."

He promises he'll send me one when he gets back to England. It arrives six weeks later in a plain brown wrapper, with a note enclosed that begins: "Dear Sweet Jew..." The show's presentation is a good one, but the paper has faded and I send it out to be re-copied. News of Tony's passing arrives before the package comes back.

I miss him.

34

SHARI AND

COMPANY

*I*F WRITING JOKES FOR A SOCK SEEMS
strange to you, believe me, it is. But
there was one sock that was delightful to write for. Lamb
Chop was the prized hand puppet of megastar Shari Lewis,
and for a while I was Lamb Chop's godfather.

I first met Shari and her friend Lamb Chop on a variety
show I was writing in Canada. Shari was a guest star. My
partner, Stan Jacobson, and I agreed she was one of the most
talented performers alive. I don't think we wrote particularly well for her, but I was sure that somewhere down the
line we'd meet again.

Somewhere down the line turns out to be three years
later, in 1966, at a family amusement park in Beverly Hills.
I was taking my five-year-old son, David, for a pony ride.
Shari has her five-year-old, Mallory, out for the same treat.
She and her publisher husband, Jeremy Tarcher, have just
moved to L.A. from New York. Since I moved my family
there the year before, I feel like a native Los Angeleno showing the new kids around. Our two families get along quite

well, and before long we're exchanging dinner invitations. Shari and I become sometime collaborators on network sit-coms and produce a number of ambitious home videos for the MGM Library. We learn to trust each other over the years and enjoy working together, though it is usually for short periods of time and often when I'm working on another job. But it isn't till the early 1990s that we get to work together full-time, on a project that lasts nearly a decade.

Shari calls one morning. Early. Shari is an early riser, so it's no surprise.

"PBS just bought my series," she says, "and we're shooting it in Canada. I need a Canadian producer—got any ideas?"

I'm still half asleep: "Sure," I say. "Stan Jacobson's still up there. Good guy, talented, he'll be perfect."

She thanks me, she hangs up, and I go back to sleep.

When I wake up, I can barely recall the conversation. But as the fog clears, I find myself wondering why she didn't ask *me*—I'm Canadian.

Next morning, she calls again. Even earlier. "I thought about it," she says. "Stan's good, but you're better. Will you do it?"

"Sure," I say, "but can we do lunch first?" Anything to get her off the phone. I go back to sleep, we do lunch, and 4½ years and five Emmy nominations later (I win one, and Shari gets three or four for Best Children's Performer), *Lamb Chop's Play-Along* finally goes off the air. It is a highly successful collaboration. And what a wild ride!

CHILDREN'S SHOWS DON'T pay very well. They're not on in prime time, so their budgets are never huge. Especially PBS children's shows. But when I sit down with Jon Slan, head of Paragon Entertainment, Shari's financial partner, he shocks me with how little money PBS is paying for the show. "Can't do it for that," I tell him. "I'm good with money, but not that good."

But Jon's a smart man. And knowledgeable. "Do the best you can. We'll bankroll you. Maybe we'll recoup from foreign sales and merchandising." He is prescient. The sale of videocassettes from the series more than makes up for our deficit. And Lamb Chop dolls sell like hotcakes at Christmastime. Millions of dollars out of merchandising. But that was the norm for children's television. They tell me the producers of that Barney series—you know, the purple dinosaur that sings those insipid kids' songs—the producers *gave* the show to PBS. I mean free! And made millions on the sale of their merchandise. Oh, well...

We go into production without a linear script. Shari has sold PBS a show based on a bunch of interactive ideas. They're good, but it's not a show yet.

"What's the overriding concept?" I ask her, first day.

"*I am,*" she says.

Not good enough. So we add some unifying ideas, some continuity, some glue—like knock-knock jokes in a front-door setting—recurring through the show. And Lamb Chop's Playhouse, a mini–comic soap opera in three acts, featuring typical kid-growing-up stories—first day at a new school, making the baseball team, buying a new dress for the party—a beginning, middle, and end, in three acts. We hope these things will hold the show together. In addition, of course, to Shari's crisp narration.

We go into production praying. We shoot the exteriors in Shari's backyard; the interiors, in a broken-down studio in Vancouver. Great town, Vancouver. We shoot thirty episodes fast and furious for six frantic weeks and still don't know what we have when I take the pieces into editing. Suspense. What comes out surprises everyone—especially me. Somehow I've put it together. With John Christie, a great editor. It is wonderful! PBS acts like they knew it all along, but they didn't, really. Jon Slan breathes a sigh of a relief when he sees the budget figures. And the rest of us get our first night's sleep in $3\frac{1}{2}$ months.

SO THAT'S THE drill for four seasons. Two months of prep—designing sets and costumes, booking studios and production personnel—but mostly, stockpiling scripts with a fabulous team of writers—Aubrey Tadman, Ken Steele, Norman Martin (who wrote that fabulous "Song That Doesn't End"), Lan O'Kun, and, of course, Shari's daughter, Mallory. She is all grown up now, a very talented young woman. She is my right hand throughout the series, and she flourishes. Tough to work for your parent. I couldn't.

After prep comes two months of solid production—rehearsing and shooting—with editing overlapping the last month of shooting. A short, compressed shooting schedule because our budget doesn't allow for a long one. Shari and I are in the studio from eight thirty in the morning till six thirty at night. We have dinner, then she goes off to study tomorrow's script, and I go edit, often past midnight. Guest stars are great—Dom DeLuise, Diana Krall, Alan Thicke, and others—marvelous staff of overworked, underpaid, talented people. They do it all with good humor. Maybe because no one has time to bitch.

I remember getting to Shari's office at nine thirty in the morning. Shari has already been working for a couple of hours with our overburdened music director, John Rodby. "Morning, John," I say, cheerily. John doesn't look up, just continues copying voluminous notes from his meeting and in that droll voice of his, remarks: "Oh, hi, Bern. I've said some very nice things about you in my suicide note." John is a brilliant musician. And, need I say, a very funny man.

LEARNING TO PRODUCE a show with puppets is a trip, totally different from anything I've ever done. More difficult, more time-consuming. The simplest things are hard. If you want an actor to walk through a door, you yell, "Walk through that door," and chances are he'll do it. You tell that to a puppet, and nothing happens. To get a puppet to walk through a door, you need two or three puppeteers, rods to move his arms, and someone to give voice to his breathless grunts. All this takes time, patience, and coordination to establish the sense of reality that some, if not all, actors give you in a flash. And those poor puppeteers—working down below the tables that puppet sets are built on. You have no idea how uncomfortable it gets. Or how close together they have to work—positively intimate. Pat Brymer, Gord Robertson—great puppeteers.

Shari is a great puppeteer, too. And ventriloquist. No one ever catches her with her lips moving. Not a problem for the Muppets, because none of their puppeteers are on camera. But Shari is a genius. She brings those little sock creatures to full life.

See, no one gives her credit for it, but Shari Lewis was a super good actor. Each character she played was perfectly defined, and she was always in character and consistently believable. She could do realistic conversations between Lamb Chop and Hush Puppy or Charlie Horse without missing a beat. Amazing. And on the rare occasion that she slipped, we were there to catch it. She never moved forward without my silent okay that the last take was worthy. It's wonderful to have that kind of trust in a relationship. And a handpicked support staff that never lets you down. Grâce à Dieu!

IN ADDITION TO producing thirty-plus episodes a year, we also did some damn good holiday specials for PBS. One, in particular, I recall, because the cast was such a wonderfully diverse group.

It's a celebration of Hanukkah, the Jewish festival of the lights. We've promised PBS three guest stars—a tough order on our budget—and we promise they'll be ethnically diverse. So the first actor I call is Pat Morita, coming off a great performance as Mister Miyagi in the hit film *Karate Kid*. I don't know Pat, but I manage to get his home phone number, call it, and leave a message on his machine: "Pat," I say, "this is Bernie Rothman, Shari Lewis's producer. We're putting together a Hanukkah special for PBS and, of course, your name sprang to mind." Figure I'd get a chuckle from him.

When he calls back, he leaves a ten-minute message on my voice mail—in fluent Yiddish!

So, okay, one guest star set; I need two more. I call Lloyd Bochner, that dashing Shakespearean actor—he'll be good contrast. Lloyd, you'll remember as Joan Collins's wicked lover in *Dynasty*. What I remember is Lloyd Bochner as my dramatics counselor at summer camp when I was eleven. Directed me in a British potboiler called *Shivering Shocks!* Absolutely launched my career! So how could Lloyd turn me down, even for PBS's stingy money? He doesn't.

For our third guest, I call Alan Thicke, 'cause he's a shoo-in. Alan is featured in a long-running sitcom at this time, and I see him as a very underestimated comic-character actor. He's already been nominated for an Emmy Award for the role of the Wolf in my production of *Trial of Red Riding Hood*. So I have to be his good luck charm—he won't let me down.

"Hi, Alan, it's Bernie..."

"Yeah, whaddya want?"

"We're doing another PBS special, Shari and I want you to guest..."

"Is the money any better?"

"It's the same," I say, and I'm listening to a click followed by a dial tone.

Two minutes later Alan calls back: "Okay, I'll do it. What's the part?"

"I think you'll like it. He's a bit of a rake..."

"Oh, I'm playing *me* again," he says.

I laugh.

"Okay, Rothman, but you owe me," he says meaningfully.

I agree: "I'll send you a case of good Bordeaux."

"More than that. It's gotta be something bigger."

"Like what?" I ask.

"A car," he says. "A Mercedes."

I hang up on him. He calls back again: "Okay, a case of wine—but not that cheap stuff!"

"You got it," I say, which I rarely do, and he finishes me off with: "And do me a favor—don't call again till you got real money!"

See? Show business can be so gratifying when you work with friends. By the way, they were all terrific, and the show is an "evergreen." Which means it'll be around at least a hundred more years, when maybe PBS will play it again.

THE END OF the story about this remarkable woman is sad. Shari and her partners decide to do a new series, far more ambitious than Lamb Chop's: *The Charlie Horse Music Pizza*.

Rather than a straight variety show to be shot in pieces and assembled in the editing room, this new one is a "book" show—a complete story, with original songs that further the plot. Tough series. Like doing a Broadway musical every week. Shari brings me what she thinks is wonderful news: PBS is ordering forty episodes, to be delivered that first season. Grim.

"Not with me producing," I tell her.

Shari is shocked. "Why not?" she demands.

" 'Cause it'll kill us," I say. "Like Lamb Chop almost did, and this one's twice as tough."

So Shari goes back to PBS, revises the delivery schedule to twenty per year, and I agree to produce the first year; Mallory, the second. It'll be murder. Tough in the writing, tough in production, tough in postproduction. We get it done, and it's a slick show. But we're wiped. Did Shari know how much the show would take out of her? Don't know. But I knew. Shari never lets little details get in her way. Details like life and death. She's determined to be on the air again at all costs. And, tragically, she is.

She goes into her second year with a great staff. She's got Mallory, she's got Shawn Williamson—possibly the finest production manager/line producer I've ever worked with—and she's got the same great writers and puppeteers. It's gonna be great.

But it isn't. In the second year, Shari is diagnosed with uterine cancer but she won't quit. By the third week of shooting, the cancer is taking its toll and they have to shut down. For the first time in her professional life, Shari Lewis has nothing left to give.

She dies a few weeks later.

Shari Lewis left behind a substantial legacy—a great library of shows and books, a brilliant young daughter, an adoring husband, a devoted manager, and all the future generations of children who might one day be lucky enough to see her shows.

Maybe the greatest kids' show performer who ever lived. What a privilege it was working with her. Makes me sad that she's gone. And how do you replace the irreplaceable?

35

MY OLD MAN,
MY OLD LADY

*E*DITING MY WAY OUT OF SHARI Lewis into Burt Reynolds. What a deal! The edit bay in Vancouver is dark—the new machines are more complex, more electronic than I'm used to—and my favorite editor, John Christie, is getting grumpier by the minute. Seems he's got a new girlfriend and our late-night hours are interfering with his sex life. Phone rings. I answer it, 'cause John's making an edit. It's my stepmother.

"Hope I didn't disturb you," says Eileen, "but it's important."

"No problem," I answer, slightly alarmed. "Anything wrong? How's Dad?"

"Fine, fine. I'm giving him a birthday party on the seventeenth—it's a Saturday, and he wants you to come in."

I think. "Gosh, Eileen—that's just two weeks off, and I'll be between two shows..."

"Well, you wouldn't want to disappoint your father, Bernie. It's his seventieth..."

I can hear my father nattering in the background as I say,

"I know, Eileen, but I'd have to take the night owl Friday night and come back Sunday. I'm going to be too tired to start my new show Monday morning."

Dad grabs the phone away from her: "Listen, I want you to come in. The whole family's coming."

"Dad, I don't know if I can..."

"Listen," he says, slightly annoyed, "it's my seventieth birthday. It's important."

I'm annoyed, too: "Hey, I just passed my fortieth—I don't remember getting so much as a card from you!"

Silence. Then, "But this is my seventieth. It's a *millstone!*"

This brings a smile to my lips. "All right, Dad, I'll come in. For a *millstone* I'll come in."

And I do. Great party!

IN THE AUTUMN of 1981 my father has a stroke. My stepmother calls to tell me—it's a mild one, not to worry, he'll be fine. I don't believe her.

My father hasn't been the same since he retired seven years ago. He sold his textile business, his apartment buildings, and moved to West Palm Beach. No one knows exactly why. Except me. I know.

"Why're you retiring?" I ask at the time. My father's life was his work.

"Why? Because I finally got it through my seventy-year-old head that you're not coming back into the business!"

"What're you going to do?"

"What am I going to do? I'll take it easy. Eileen and I will travel—I'll enjoy myself. Don't you think I've earned the right?"

"Yes, Dad, you've earned the right. But you're not fooling me a bit. You know no one in Florida. You don't even like Florida."

After his stroke, I call every day to check on him. He isn't getting any better; he's getting worse. He slips into a coma.

I GO STRAIGHT to the hospital when I arrive in Palm Beach. My father is lying on the bed in his nightshirt, tubes coming out of every orifice in his body. He is motionless but for his heavy breathing.

I pull up a chair and begin talking to him—just him and me, having a conversation in the lonely room. It's kind of one-sided. But although he doesn't respond, I know he can hear me. People in comas can. So I just prattle on, gossiping about show business, giving him the latest about Mel and Renee, hoping that eventually I'll get through to him.

After two full days of talking to his motionless body, I get mad. My father is hiding from me—I'm sure of it. He's telling me to leave him alone, let him die in peace. It seems to me a very spiteful thing for him to do.

I GO TO a phone booth, call my brother and my sister, tell them what I think—our father has decided to "take a cab," and if they want to say goodbye to him, they'd better hurry on down to Florida. They both promise to fly in that evening. I go back into my father's room, distraught, discouraged, and mad as hell.

I start yelling: "Listen, Dad, you're in big trouble now. I just spoke to your beautiful daughter and your son the judge. They're both on their way down here, and you better be up by the time they arrive!"

I walk out of the room, thoroughly pissed off, and get into my father's beat-up old Pontiac. I head for the I-95, drive up and down the Florida coast for what must be three or four hours.

This is my first trip to the citrus state, and I don't like it any better than I thought I would. The scenery is drab and low-lying, lots of motels, and where there should have been something to see, the views are blocked by gaudy road signs. Oh, sure, there are palm trees everywhere. But there's a gray sameness to it all—even the ubiquitous golf courses seem lacking in color. What a monotonous drive! I keep waiting for that broad glimpse of the turquoise sea, a white sandy beach, or a marina scattered with lovely sailboats—something to lift my spirits. Where on earth are those picturesque locations we see every week on *Miami Vice*? Not there!

Still, the drive gives me a chance to clear my head and think about all the things my father has and hasn't been for me over the years. What a strong man he's been—that's what he demanded of us and of himself. He was an amazing man—dauntless, tireless, unswerving. And I'm about to lose him. He's been slipping away since he retired—his hearing has faded, his vision, his sharpness. He doesn't want to hang around and be less of a man than he's been all his life.

When I get back to his hospital room, he's up, out of his coma, and yelling at the nurse.

"Get me up, get me up!" he shouts. The poor nurse, terrified, is tying a sash around his chest, holding him firm against the mattress of the bed, which she's cranked to an upright position. And someone else is in the room now—a Bible-toting priest is watching the proceedings. "It's a miracle," he says softly to me, "a miracle . . ." I think he came to administer last rites. But I know better. The "miracle" is my father's stubbornness. He does exactly what he wants, and what he wants is to say good-bye.

"Dad, you're up," I say, beaming.

My father beams back. "I'm a man of iron!" he says proudly, talking from the side of his semiparalyzed mouth with great effort. He *is* a man of iron.

MY SISTER AND brother arrive late that night, and my stepmother shows us what rooms we're to sleep in. My brother and I share a bedroom for the first time since I was twelve. I didn't like sharing a bedroom with Mel when we were kids. He was a compulsive reader, and his reading kept me up all night. But I don't mind sharing on this occasion. I'm feeling pretty tentative, and my older brother's steadiness calms my nerves. We talk about Dad until dawn.

When we get to the hospital the following morning, my father's already up and glowing. It's a very happy reunion, for him and for us. Dad is now speaking with less effort, and Renee is somewhat relieved—maybe her father will survive after all. Much emotion and affection among us. Mel and Dad, who have often been at odds, are very sweet to each other. And of course, Renee—always warm and wonderful, everybody's darling, is the family glue.

When I leave the following day to get back to the show I'm producing, everyone is happy. And I feel I'm leaving my father in very good hands. He thinks so, too. It's a high note.

My siblings stay on for two more days. Dad dies the day after they leave.

My father was a family man. To his dying day. Tough! But he did some wonderful things for his kids. And I'll always be grateful to him for coming out of that deep coma to say good-bye to us.

MY MOM'S GOODBYE takes a little longer. She's in an assisted-living residence in Toronto and actually liking it. Takes years to persuade her to move in, but with Renee nearby, and full-time help, she's pleased to be free of looking after herself. Only problem is, they won't let her smoke. Which is probably why she doesn't move in in the first place. Until then, my mother smokes three and a half packs a day. On her eightieth birthday I ask her: "Mom—when are you going to give up smoking?"

"Soon as George Burns does," she says.

At age eighty-nine, my mother finally gives up her search for the ideal husband and goes gently into that good night.

Her contribution to my life has been incalculable. I'm even willing to overlook the piano lessons. The love of music and art and ballet and opera and theater and literature have all come with her encouragement. If my father has instilled us with ambition and drive and the will to succeed in life, it's my mother who enriches our lives and creates an environment of beauty and culture. So, notwithstanding our parents' bickering, we all learn to laugh together. That's what we do every night at the dinner table—we argue and we laugh. The humor and intelligence our parents have surrounded us with is our legacy. And we'll cherish it all our lives.

36

BURT

REYNOLDS—

LIVE!

*W*E DID TWO SHOWS WITH BURT. Ninety-minute late-night specials for NBC. First one was very special, very gripping. We took Burt to Leavenworth Penitentiary, and did a show for the inmates. Tell you more about that later.

The second Burt Reynolds special—*Burt and the Girls*—is Burt's idea. He sees himself as an ace at the art of improvisation. I give him no more than a seven. But we book a bevy of Hollywood's best actress/improvisers, each to play a scene opposite Burt. Carol Burnett, Nancy Dussault, Della Reese, Joyce Van Patten, Bernadette Peters—all take a shot at it. Bravely. The girls are all brilliant improvisers. The show, "live" on videotape, takes six hours to shoot. And seven weeks in the editing room to pull together. With a very great editor. Inch by inch. Henry Jaffe, the wry and wily executive producer whose money we are spending, calls every day.

"What are you guys doing in there?"

"Saving your ass, Henry," I say laughing.

And he says, "My ass is fine, thank you; it doesn't need saving. How about saving what little is left of my money?"

In the end, I think we did a pretty good ass-saving job. The show ends up looking just fine, gets a forty "share" thanks to Burt's popularity (he was a number-one box office attraction at the time), and Mr. Reynolds's reputation as an ace improviser remains intact. Ha!

Show folk are evenly divided. There are those who don't know. And there are those who don't know they don't know. Burt Reynolds doesn't know he doesn't know. Makes it difficult.

I always figure myself to be in the first group. I know I don't know. In show business, you *can't* know. It's like baseball—nobody bats a thousand. If you can take a good swing at the ball, try not to strike out too often, and once in a while hit a home run, then you're doing better than most. I was born with good theatrical sense. But nobody I know, knows. Not even Burt.

BURT REYNOLDS AT LEAVENWORTH is a smashing show. We take Dinah Shore with us (she's living with Burt at the time), country singer Merle Haggard, and Jonathan Winters, and entertain two audiences full of inmates (five or six hundred in all). In addition, there are five inmate acts who entertain beautifully, and a prison band put together by John Rodby, Dinah's exceptional music director. It takes John three solid weeks of rehearsing, but in the end, they sound pretty good. And the crew—stagehands, lighting guys, and so on—work wonders under our department heads. The only thing I don't care for about the whole three-week experiment is the food. It's awful. But what can you expect from a maximum-security federal penitentiary—caviar and champagne?

Burt is terrific for our whole stay in the prison. He talks with the inmates, schmoozes with them, plays football with them—he's just great. So when it comes time to do the show, he's totally at ease as a host with the inmates, and they're at ease with him.

I HAVE A few uneasy moments. First, when I notice the guards don't wear guns. This, we are told, is so that in case of a riot or any other disturbance, the prisoners can't swipe the guards' weapons. Reassuring.

Second is the upstairs lounge. For the hour or two we spend with the inmates relaxing between rehearsals, we're locked in. Without guards. Pool tables, Ping-Pong—all very nice. But scary. Then I notice I'm the last man there—locked in with Big Jim Wakefield, the prison's tough guy, a lifer who all but runs the prison. He notices it too. And suggests he should be performing a second song on the show. I take a deep breath and say no. The show is already too long. He scowls. My knees are knocking. And before he can slit my throat, I hurry out the gate.

THEN THERE IS the interruption between audiences. One of the prison gangs gets out of hand. So the show is delayed an hour or so. Have to empty out the theater.

Johnny Winters arrives late to the show. In the middle, to be exact. We know in advance, of course, but his manager requests that I meet him at the guard gate. I do. He is pale, frightened out of his wits as we walk down the prison hallway, eyed by prisoners on both sides, both of us more than a little nervous. Whew!

BOBBY AND JED are the best of the prison acts. They sing, they play, they write their own music. Two sensitive young men who sing beautiful love songs, in prison for God knows what reason. So we get them sprung early, find a manager for them, book them a few gigs. They're back in the slammer six months later. One for breaking parole, the other for stabbing a guy in a bar.

WHEN THE SHOW is over, we're all invited to the warden's house for a late supper. Well, not all of us. Just some of us. The rest have to stay behind, can't come to the wrap party. Sad. But I never met an inmate who admitted he was in prison for good reason.

37

BEAM
ME UP,
BILLY

*W*HEN I WAS A RELUCTANT STUDENT
in business at McGill, I remember
hitchhiking a ride down to college one day and the conversation I had with a friend's father, who picked me up.

"So what are you doing after you graduate?" he asks.

"Family business," I reply. "Dad's in textiles."

"Smart boy," he says to me. "I wish you'd talk to my son. Can you believe it? He wants to be an actor. Crazy business. He could come into my business—the pants business—make a good living the rest of his life. But no—he's gotta be an actor. And starve!"

"Well, Mr. Shatner," I say, "you never know."

My brother, Mel, and William Shatner were summer camp counselors together in 1948. I was just a kid. But on their day off Mel would bring his friends to our country place for dinner—we had a Chinese cook—and that's when I met Bill.

Handsome, charming, and lots of fun was Billie, an aspiring actor. When I entered McGill a few years later, he was "Mr. Theater" on campus. He was talented, a fine and versatile actor. I wasn't sure he'd become a big star, but he certainly was determined to be one. To his credit, he never stopped trying. I believe he earned his star on the Hollywood Walk of Fame, as well as the many millions of dollars his detractors said he'd never make.

But Bill had another passion in those days, and her name was Gisela. She was bright and pretty and lots of fun. This might have been puppy love, but they adored each other.

Bill and I crossed paths a few years later. It was 1956. I had a theater in Toronto, and Bill was courting Gloria, a lovely actress in my cast. By then, he was a well-established actor. He had done leads at the Stratford Festival and lots of guest-starring roles on television. Bill was well on his way.

He and Gloria got married, moved to the States, and started raising a family. I'd run into them from time to time when I first moved to California in the mid '60s. They had three beautiful little girls and a family life to go with Shatner's skyrocketing career. But the marriage didn't last. Bill was achieving his career goals, but, like many of us in the entertainment community, he paid a price for it. Home life came second. Professionally, he was everywhere. Turn on the TV, he was there in a series. Go to the movies, Bill dominated the screen. William Shatner was becoming a household name.

Hard to say what Shatner's big break was. Was it playing those heroic Shakespearean roles at Stratford? Certainly helped develop his style. Or was it that fine performance in *Suzie Wong* on Broadway, where he showed what he could do with a romantic role? Was it his star turn on *Star Trek*? The character he created—Captain Kirk—was unique and enduring. *T.J. Hooker,* a hit series, ran longer than *Star Trek*. Bill was playing a less complex character, and why not? Could Shatner play a cop? Sure. Shatner could play anything.

And he did. Just look at the lawyer he created for *Boston Legal*. Brilliant! And those commercials he did for that Internet travel company. Hilarious! Then, the man goes on late-night television and *sings!* He's relentlessly versatile—a one-man cast of thousands. What was William Shatner's big break? His big break was never quitting. And he never will.

Bill married several times. Yes, yes, he's something of a romantic. After all, he grew up in Montreal, a French city, where romance is encouraged. No, it's not encouraged, it's compulsory. One of his marriages ended tragically. Early on, Bill's wife drowned in their swimming pool.

Wow! The papers were all over it. Where was Shatner at the time? How come he wasn't home? How could she drown in her own pool? She was a good swimmer. Had she been drinking? The media can be very cruel.

I meant to call Bill at the time, offer my condolences and support. I tell him that a year or so later when I run into him on Ventura Boulevard outside his daughter's boutique. We hug warmly, as old friends do, and he leads me over to the nearby Starbucks (there's a Starbucks nearby everywhere), and we talk. I tell him how sorry I am, that I should have called. He is gracious about it, and we talk for a long time about the old days in Montreal.

"Whatever happened to Gisela?" I ask.

Bill shrugs. "Married my cousin Arthur."

"Nice girl," I say.

"Yeah, nice girl."

A very attractive woman joins us at our table.

"You're late," says Shatner, "and that's supposed to be the star's prerogative." They laugh, and Bill introduces me to the lady. She's charming.

"You an actor, too?" I ask her.

"Nope. I'm in the horse business."

"Oh, of course," I say, remembering that Bill's hobby is show horses. "So you two are doing business together."

"Actually, Bernie, we're getting married," says Bill.

"Really," I say, needling him, 'cause I think he's joking. "And have we set a date?"

Bill smiles. "Tuesday," he says, and they're laughing again, playing the love game like a couple of teenagers.

I get up to leave, say goodbye but they're having too much fun to notice. Like I said, Bill's a romantic. Romantics are always looking for that one grand love. I think Bill found her.

Hope so.

38

TWO CEOS

SOME GUYS YOU MEET EARLY IN their careers and watch them rise to the top, like cream rises in a milk bottle. Men of destiny.

Like Leslie Moonves. My wife met Leslie before I did. At the time, he was working as a development executive for my friend Saul Ilson. He was an actor who decided not to be one. He and Saul are developing a script about psychologists, and since Bobbi is one of the best, they use her as consultant. Leslie is in his late twenties, handsome, charming, and smart. Since Bobbi is unaccustomed to those qualities at home, she is careful not to sing his praises. Hmmm...

Then I meet him. It's during my term at Twentieth Century Fox, where Leslie is in charge of TV movies. I bring him several ideas for MOWs. Some he likes; some he doesn't. He certainly leaves no doubt which is which. Never pulls punches! Don't think he knows how to. Goes to the essence of every idea, makes suggestions that are always in keeping with the spirit of the project. We go to the network with a couple—we don't sell any, but it certainly isn't for his lack of commitment. Leslie never backs down. Lets them know if they pass, they're making a mistake. That way, there'll be a little less sales resistance next time. Very, very smart fella.

It doesn't surprise me when Leslie Moonves is made president of Lorimar Television. It does surprise me when he makes me a generous offer to go with him. I'm shooting a series out of town when my secretary moves me into my new office on the lot. I can't believe it when I get there. I call Leslie: "Leslie—someone's made a mistake."

"With what?" he asks.

"This office—it's magnificent. Gotta be for someone important!"

"Are you calling to complain, Bernie?" he wants to know.

I'm flabbergasted—it's so plush, my own shower—the works! "Well, no," I say. "It's just that..."

"Good. Then just shut up. The office *is* for someone important—you!" He hangs up.

I don't do much business for Lorimar. I've begun shooting the Shari Lewis series, and that takes me out of town. But Leslie is always warm and encouraging, and to this day, we greet each other with smiles. Maybe he senses what pleasure it gives me watching his career rise. He takes Lorimar, Warner Brothers, and CBS all to the top. And with Les as CEO, CBS will always be number one.

IVAN FECAN IS the CEO of CTV, Canada's most successful television network. And if that's not enough, he presides over a dozen or so cable TV networks and a couple of national newspapers for good measure. Busy man. How'd he get there? I don't know. I can only tell you that I watched him climb from a minor post at a local TV station up through the ranks of Canadian and U.S. television to become Canada's major media czar. Am I surprised? No. Does he deserve it? Absolutely. He's brilliant. One of the most creative business minds I've ever been exposed to.

In the early '80s, whenever I visit Toronto, I have dinner with my darling Sandra Faire. Sandra was my protégé from my early producing days. She's smart, cute, and very cheeky, and I knew she'd become a great producer in no time. Which she does. On one of those dinner dates she asks if she can bring someone she's been seeing. And she does. And that would be Ivan. The three of us become close friends over dinner that first night. You can't miss the ambition in Ivan, the strategist. He is twenty-six and already knows everything. Not quite true—what little he doesn't know he wants to. Immediately. Man, he's very impressive! And, man, we have fun! From time to time he comes to L.A., and I introduce him to my friends in Tinseltown. He impresses them all.

Then one day he calls, very excited, to tell me he's just had a meeting with Brandon Tartikoff, NBC's powerful program chief.

"How'd it go?" I ask.

"I think pretty well. He says he wants to hire me. Think he means it?"

"Can't say with those guys. And I don't know him well enough to ask. But we'll think of something."

Now I swear this is true. The very next night I run into Brandon at a cocktail party. (I know, I know, it's too much of a coincidence, but I swear it happened just this way.) "So, Brandon, I hear you met a friend of mine yesterday."

"Oh yeah, Bernie? Who?" (Should have said, "Whom.")

"Ivan Fecan's his name. He's brilliant."

"Yeah, I really liked him," says Brandon. "Thinking of hiring him."

"Well Brandon, better not think too long. He met the guys at CBS, and Bud Grant loved him." It wasn't a lie—maybe a bit of an exaggeration. Brandon hires him next day. Might have anyway, but a little nudge never hurts.

A few years later, when Ivan calls to tell me he's leaving NBC to take the top programming job at CBC, I tell him he's leaving too soon. He pays no attention to me. So we go out and get roaring drunk together. Of course, he makes the right career decision. He becomes CEO of CTV, Canada's biggest commercial TV empire. And selfishly, he and Sandra and I can go right on having our elegant dinners together whenever I'm in Toronto. And Bobbi's joined the club now, too. It's a rare thing in Hollywood. A ménage à quatre!

39

THE

LUCKIEST

YEAR OF

MY LIFE

*M*Y DOCTOR GIVES IT TO ME straight. Bobbi is there to hear it, too. *Cancer,* he says. Doesn't even call it the big C, the way our parents used to. Colon cancer, advanced stage. Have to get under the knife, fast.

Bobbi and I talk about it in bed that night. All cried out, can't get to sleep.

"Whatever happens—don't let them keep me on machines. Pull the plug."

"Don't ask that—please don't ask that. It's too heavy a trip." She is weeping.

"Look," I say, taking her in my arms, "I've got five grown kids I'm proud of—they're on their way. I've had nearly thirty years doing enjoyable work, and I've managed to produce most of the shows I dreamt of. And, although it took a while, I found myself one good woman to love. That's more than most people get in a lifetime."

"Not enough," she murmurs. "Not nearly enough."

WE FIND THE surgeon we want by taking a census from our half a dozen doctor friends. Stephen Shapiro is the right guy. Cedars-Sinai's best. Good hospital, all private rooms, and food that's darn near edible. I call the kids that weekend—have to let them know. To my surprise, they all take it calmly. But I'm scared. Till I speak to Nicholas. Nick is my youngest—an all-American volleyball star in premed at the University of California at San Diego. Nerves of steel.

"The operation's Tuesday. I'll be writing again in a week," I say gamely.

But, I can't fool *him*.

"Wow, that's fast!" he answers. "Don't I even get to skip a few classes to visit you?" he cracks. Then he gets serious.

"Dad, if I'm not mistaken colon cancer has a very high rate of recovery. You're gonna be fine."

Is it true? Nick doesn't make that kind of mistake. But if it *is* true, how come Dr. Katz never said it? How come what he said sounded like a death sentence?

Two weeks later I find out. The colon tumor has metastasized, and now I need liver surgery. One chance in five I'll survive. Glad they didn't tell me that in advance.

Hey, listen—don't worry! This happened in 1988—I'm still here.

After the first operation, I'm up and around in a week. Feel great, can't figure out what all this fuss about cancer surgery is about. Plenty of chemo for the next few months (no big deal—still got my hair), and I bank several quarts of my own blood in case I need it. (Sounds a bit ghoulish, what?)

So I'm lying there on a gurney in the hospital corridor before the liver surgery. Bobbi's with me, of course, faking all the confidence in the world. And me? I'm too stupid to be scared! The doctor comes over and says, "Sorry, Mrs. Rothman, time for him to go in now."

Bobbi kisses me, and I see her eyes well up (unusual for her) as she walks away.

Then, I call out, "Bobbi—" She stops. "Don't date yet!"

And she bursts out laughing. In fact, we both do.

The second operation is quite different from the first. It takes $9\frac{1}{2}$ hours with four or five doctors to fix me up. I awake in the ICU. Well, not quite. I'm not sure whether I'm dead or alive. But, apparently, I'm alive. Still am. And six months later I'm back to normal. Or, at least, normal for me.

IT'S A YEAR after my first operation. Bobbi and I are in bed one night, and I say, "You know—I think this has been one of the best years of my life."

"You've gotta be kidding," she says.

"No, I mean it. I discovered I have some courage, I have a wonderful wife and family and friends who love me... and look—I'm still here!"

Bobbi's face is suffused with anger.

"Maybe the best for you, but the worst for the rest of us. Don't you know what it's like to lose someone you love? We almost lost you, Bern! Can you understand that?"

Yes, dear Bobbi, I can.

How lucky I am to be alive and feel the love around me. Luckiest year of my life!

40

THE

SKATERS'

WALTZ

*M*Y FIRST SHOT OUT OF THE CHUTE is a skating show. It's a challenge. Starts with a phone call from Michael Rosenberg, Elizabeth Manley's manager. He'd just closed a deal for his client to have her own skating special on CTV television. Murray Chercover, long-time president of CTV, wants us to meet. Can we discuss the possibility of my producing said special? I hate skating shows, but I need the money. Certainly, Mr. Rosenberg. The Beverly Hills Polo Lounge at five-thirty will be just fine.

He's tall, blond, handsome, from New Mexico—hardly what I expect. Doesn't even smoke cigars. But speaks in detailed clarity about this show I'm going to produce for his client. How does he know? In my expert hands, she will become a superstar. What a salesman! Meanwhile, I have no idea who his client is. Ultimately, he tells me.

Liz Manley is the darling of the '88 Winter Olympics, beating Debi Thomas, the American star, whipping the favorite, Katarina Witt, in all but the compulsories. She's a cute, blonde, ebullient twenty-two-year-old, and enters as the underdog (ranked 17th in the world). But she skates with such flair, such personality, she knocks the judges' thermal socks off. Silver medal! Canada loudly applauds its diminutive heroine—spreads her action photos on the front pages of every newspaper in the country. How could I have missed her? Rosenberg wants to know. How? Easy. I've been living outside Canada for twenty years, never been interested in Olympic competition, and grew up in Siberia-esque Montreal, where I made it a point never to step outdoors in the winter. That's how!

But, yes, Michael Rosenberg, I will produce your client's special if Murray Chercover wants me to, if Elizabeth is as charming and talented as you say, and if you and I can come to terms.

We can't come to terms. Michael thinks I'm asking too much. I'm not, and I'm not budging. Undaunted, Michael goes to the rival network, CBC, and offers them the show. Carol Reynolds, the CBC's program director, assures him she will be delighted to have the show on her network. Provided Bernie Rothman is producing. (Hmmm... Wonder why she'd say that.) Michael is furious. Goes back to CTV, complaining about my usury. Chercover, who knows my work as well as my prices, makes me part of a take-it-or-leave-it deal with his network. And Michael Rosenberg learns the hard way that despite the vastness of its territory, Canada is a very small country.

That's the last argument Michael and I ever have. We do several shows together, all of them successful. And I discover the wonderful world of skating. It's magic!

MY FIRST SKATING show with Ms. Manley is called *Dear Elizabeth*. It's based on five fan letters Liz receives after her stunning triumph at the Olympics. The letters (faked, of course) are from Christopher Plummer, Alan Thicke, Rich Little, David Foster, and the champion pairs skaters, Barbara Underhill and Paul Martini. Each of these celebrities shows up for a fun and flattering segment with Liz. Each has his or her own style, gives a polished performance. Liz, the super-star-to-be, keeps up with all of them.

Having Rich Little on your show is like having a cast of thousands. You also get Jack Benny, Johnny Carson, George Burns, Kirk Douglas, Bill Clinton, and the mayor of Ottawa (where we're shooting this show). There's no better voice impressionist than Rich. He even teaches Liz to do James Cagney.

I've known Christopher Plummer from his early acting days in Montreal, have watched him develop into an inter-national star. Chris does a piece from *Cyrano*. There's no finer actor in the world. Charms the pants off Liz. (Fortunately, she wears long johns underneath.)

Alan Thicke is his dependably funny self—mocking his own vanity (there's plenty to mock!). Then manages to lose his team's hockey match to Liz's team, which happens to include Luc Robitaille.

The pairs champions, Martini and Unterhill, are fabulous! Such grace, such style. More like flying than skating. And in those flimsy costumes on below-zero ice. Amazing! I am shocked to learn that the elegant skater Paul Martini started out to be a hockey player.

Then, there's David—dear David Foster. He's somewhat new to me. Absolute musical genius. Must've won a couple of dozen Grammy Awards since. I ask if he'll write a song for the show and sing it to Liz.

"Sure. What's she like?" he asks.

"Cute, bumptious, very unaffected," I tell him. "She can't believe all this is happening to her. Surrounded by celebrities, everyone making such a fuss over her. 'What am I doing here?' she keeps asking." Sweet.

A week later I run into David at an event in the Beverly Hills Four Seasons. "Just who I'm looking for," he says and, without another word, leads me to the cocktail lounge, where a jazz group is playing for the audience. Politely, but firmly, David asks if he can borrow their piano for a minute. No way can they refuse. David sits down and plays and sings a song for me, as if there's no one else in this crowded room. Just like in the movies. "What Am I Doing Here?" is the title of David's song. Touching, beautiful. It's the highlight of what is to be a very entertaining television show. CTV's highest-rated special of the year. I even liked the skating!

I SPEND A lot of CTV's money on *Dear Elizabeth*. More than they're willing to spend on a second year's special.

So that other network—CBC—makes us an offer we can't refuse.

Liz is rapidly becoming a TV star, gaining in confidence every day. I determine that our second show isn't to be a boring old skating show. This year we'll do an original musical comedy on ice. Talk about chutzpah! I write a story outline and a couple of songs and take them to Carol Reynolds, the CBC's program director. She loves the idea. "But Liz isn't an actress," she says. "Do you think she can handle this stuff?"

"With the right director, she can," I tell her, and I call my friend Burt Metcalfe.

Burt produced *M*A*S*H* for most of its life and directed many of its episodes. He's wonderful with actors—had been an actor himself—so if anyone can teach Liz how to act, he's the guy. Besides, the part she'll be playing won't take much acting. Maybe none at all. It calls for a bumptious tomboy in the leading role. *Back to the Beanstalk* is the title, and Liz Manley was born to play the part of Jack.

Getting Burt to direct isn't easy. He's never directed a musical before, much less a musical on ice. He feels he's a bad risk. I point out that the great British film musical *Oliver* was directed by Sir Carol Reed, who couldn't even whistle a tune. (Don't know if that's true, but it worked.) Next day Burt calls back and says yes.

He does wonders with Liz. A great director is a great director in any medium. Also great is Sandra Bezic, the world's finest skating choreographer, who always contributes creatively. We have a super cast of character actors, led by the late, great Heath Lamberts, a Shakespearean, who plays a giant, undersized because his wife has forced him onto a vegetarian diet. The show is nominated for a Gemini Award and plays happily on the Disney Channel forever after!

I WON'T BORE you with details of the sequel we do with Liz, *The Trial of Red Riding Hood*. It's a grander show—"a trial of the century" set in the Klondike, 1899. Red Riding Hood is on trial for wolficide. It features the Three Rappin' Pigs, a tough ol' Grannie, and Alan Thicke, who's brilliant in his portrayal of the Wolf (everyone says he was typecast). The show plays for years around the world. And a funny thing happens to us on the way to Grandma's house. We win the Gemini for Best Musical Special of the Year. Now, who's afraid of that?

I REMEMBER READING in *People* magazine in the early '70s that Tai Babilonia made an attempt on her own life. Everyone knew Tai and Randy—"America's sweethearts." At a time when the Russians dominated pairs figure skating with their tall, muscular male skaters and diminutive female partners, Tai and Randy changed the style. They were perfectly matched in size and they were beautiful. They won the Worlds, and they did it all with finesse. I wonder what dire circumstance would motivate a beautiful young woman like Tai to want to end it all. She seemed to have the world at her fingertips.

Michael Rosenberg comes up with an answer:

Tai and Randy, who were Michael's clients, had a meteoric rise in the skating world. They were odds-on favorites to win the Olympic gold. In practice on the day before the competition, Randy severely pulls a hamstring. Game over. Michael insists Tai never recovered from that crushing disappointment. I don't buy it.

Tai Babilonia is doomed from age four. She loves skating. Her parents see how talented she is. They invest everything in Tai's career and push her the rest of her life. Correction. She has no life. None without her skates on. When Tai isn't in school, she's on ice. Practicing, for hours and hours and hours. Being both a pleaser and a perfectionist, she can never allow herself failure. So when Randy is injured and they can't compete, Tai Babilonia feels she's failed. Her life is over. There are rumors of substance abuse at the time. I don't know or care. But if she was using, it was more a symptom of her unhappiness than a cause.

Michael sold the movie rights to NBC the week the *People* magazine article appeared. Brought me in as the producer. We did the story of Tai and Randy's rise to fame and Randy's terrible accident that led to Tai's downfall. NBC seemed pleased with the film, but I wasn't. We never got beneath the skin of the character. Sad, because there was an important personal story to tell.

Skaters, like dancers and fashion models, have to sacrifice everything for their careers. They starve themselves to look good, train endlessly, work like slaves for recognition. If they do make it, fame is short lived. In the meantime, their youth is gone and they have little to show for it. They pay an overwhelming price for their art. Their families, too, make big sacrifices. Their careers are expensive ones, so only wealthy families can comfortably afford them. Most skaters are from middle-class homes, so it's a struggle. Tai's dad was a cop—which means scrimping and saving. Siblings usually get shortchanged. Tough stuff.

Tai Babilonia is a remarkable woman. Bright and warm, beautiful and funny. And very, very talented. But beyond the barest necessities, she never learns how to ask for what she wants. Doesn't think she deserves it. So busy pleasing others, she never figures out what she wants for herself.

I remember driving her home from rehearsal in my little sports car one night. I did a Henry Higgins routine: "You've got to ask for what you want, Tai. Otherwise, you'll never have a life."

"I know, I know. But there's so much I need..."

"No, Tai, not 'need.' 'Want.' You've got to find out what you want, and ask for it."

"Sure, okay, I will..." she says wistfully.

"Let me hear you say it. Say, 'I want.'"

Tai stares at me. Then, hesitantly: "I w-want. Okay?" She's uncomfortable.

"Say it again. A few times."

Pause. Enunciates, carefully: "I want... I want... I want..."

"Great. Now you've got to find something you want. And tell me about it."

Tai gazes, looking around for something to want. "I want... I want... I want... I want your Porsche!" She giggles with delight. She gets the point.

Last I saw Tai was with Randy at their book signing a few years ago. Good friends, good partners for decades. She looks happy. She has a little boy—Scout—bright and beautiful like his mama. She designs lovely jewelry, teaches, writes children's books, performs, lives with a very nice man. She's got a life. She wants one.

41

WHAT

AN ACTOR,

WHAT

A MEAL

*B*EST ACTOR I EVER WORKED WITH was Christopher Plummer. Not that he did his best acting with me—in fact, we never did a play together. But if you ever saw him on stage—and I have many times—you'd know he was the best. Right up there with Lawrence Olivier, John Gielgud, and the rest of the classical rat pack. I saw him do *Hamlet* at Stratford and understood the character and the play for the first time. Following night he played Sir Andrew Aguecheek opposite Doug Campbell's Falstaff—they were zany as any vaudeville team. Big laughs, great theater! Not that there was anything wrong with Chris's work in film, such as *The Sound of Music,* to name but a few. It's just that Shakespeare wrote more interesting characters than Oscar Hammerstein.

I knew Christopher Plummer growing up in Montreal, and we saw each other once in a while over the years. He made his reputation early, and we all knew he was destined for stardom. I always dreamt of doing a musical *Cyrano de*

Bergerac with Chris on television but could never talk my bosses into it. Not commercial, they insisted. Maybe. But first time I got Plummer to do a TV guest shot for me, he performed an excerpt from *Cyrano* that was so moving the audience gave him an ovation that went on forever.

Chris cohosted a special I produced for Mila Mulroney, wife of Canada's former prime minister, Brian Mulroney. Chris and Stefanie Powers were wonderful together. It was one of those hands-across-the-border evenings, with a glitzy marquee that included Melissa Manchester, Cirque du Soleil, Hume Cronyn, Jessica Tandy, Celine Dion, and many others. Barbara Bush, the U.S. first lady at the time, was guest of honor.

Celine, just coming into her own, sang one of her big, dramatic ballads, and anyone who didn't know of her then wouldn't soon forget her. Hume and Jessica, always polished and sophisticated, did a wonderful piece about a married couple fighting over a game of Scrabble. And the clowns from Cirque, unknown at the time, were their brilliant, hilarious selves.

I wrote a piece for Plummer I hoped would cement relations. It was called "The Eagle and the Beaver," and Chris performed it with great wit and charm. It was actually a parable about the differences in our two countries—the proud, high-flying eagle and the industrious beaver, a blue-collar sort of fellow—and how they work to help each other in times of trouble. I don't know that it cemented relations, but it didn't do them any harm. Certainly, war did not break out between the two countries. Chris was fabulous and the audience loved it.

My fondest memory is the event after the show. I was an honored guest at a state banquet, with Stefanie Powers on my left and Barbara Bush on my right. Seated opposite the Canadian prime minister. Dinner was pheasant under glass. Now what the hell was I doing in that company?

Ran into Plummer some months later, on a street in downtown Toronto.

"Mr. Producer," he says—probably momentarily forgot my name. "I owe you a dinner."

"Oh, no, Chris, I..."

"I really do. That state banquet you got me to was magnificent! Tomorrow night okay for you?"

"Well, I... sure, fine."

"I found this great restaurant—just opened," he says, and we set the date.

I am dumbfounded. Actors don't usually invite producers to dinner. Especially famous actors. So I go the following night, cheerful, but mindful that every time I have dinner with an actor I wind up paying.

The restaurant is gorgeous, and the meal that Plummer has preordered is magnificent. Course after course, accompanied by the finest of French wines. I can see the bill mounting up astronomically, but I think, oh well, it's dinner with Plummer. No matter what this costs me, it will be worth it. It's a great meal with a very charming man, and I'll have this story to tell.

Surprise! After a sumptuous dessert with brandy, Chris picks up the tab, pays it with a smile. Probably the best meal I've ever had, to say nothing of the company.

No wonder he's my favorite actor!

42

A BRIGHT,

SHINING

STAR

I'VE SAVED THE BEST FOR THE LAST. David Suzuki is my favorite star on this planet (I've got a few others on Saturn). The work he's done on behalf of Mother Earth is prodigious and remarkable. It makes me think we've still got a chance.

What's most remarkable is how he started. Suzuki spent four of his precious formative years in an internment camp in British Columbia. You see, his *grandparents* were Japanese. Most of us, had we been snatched from our homes and forced into isolation, would have become embittered the rest of our lives. But not David. He fell in love with the planet during those years and has been dedicated to protecting it ever since. Thank God! Our species has been so arrogant in the use and abuse of our environment that it has taken the inspired leadership of a few wise and dedicated people like Suzuki to begin to turn things around. He's been doing it on TV, on radio, in lecture halls, on campuses—for over forty years. And, I suspect, it's just a beginning. Now that's a star!

Meeting Suzook came as a result of a phone call from a group of his friends who were trying to put together a

Suzuki evening in Hollywood. John Candy, Dan Aykroyd, David Foster, and others had all grown up with David's long-running TV series, *The Nature of Things*. But they wanted their U.S. colleagues to know David better and to join in the battle to preserve the planet. These evenings cost money, and after a year of talking about it, they hadn't raised any.

So I had lunch with Suzuki and the people who ran his foundation, the David Suzuki Foundation. I was shocked. They weren't academics or enviromaniacs. They were just charming, everyday people. Oh, sure, they knew the facts: Who was clear-cutting our forests. Who was polluting our air, our rivers, our lakes. But most of those facts were available to all of us. And most of us, including our politicians, know what has to be done to reverse the eco-damage. So how are these Suzuki people different? They walk the talk, that's how.

In addition to the work they do to pro-activate this planet's return to normalcy, they live their lives that way. They drive hybrid cars, they conserve energy in every way, they recycle paper, wood, garbage, metal—everything. They deal with other animals—wild and domesticated—as cohabitants of our planet. That's what David and Tara and Viki Wilson, and Jim Fulton, and the others, do every day of their lives. So do David's lovely daughters Severn and Sarika, who've joined in the fray. So maybe there's hope for the planet. They fight all the bad guys—the factories that spew out carbon emissions, the car companies that sell gas-guzzlers, the lumber companies that won't respect old-growth forests and the fauna that inhabit them, the oil companies that drill indiscriminately, and on and on. And they all lead rich lives and lead us in directions where our lives will be richer, too. And where our planet will be healthier, and our grandchildren will enjoy living here, just as we have.

David Suzuki has been awarded fifteen honorary doctor-ates. Must be a reason. And all those other prizes his TV series keeps winning. Must be a reason. And those hun-dreds of sold-out speaking engagements. Must be a reason. There is—he has a nice way of telling people what's good for them. (Remember how much trouble our mothers had getting us to eat our broccoli?) David is our mentor, our leader, our shining star.

But what I like most about working with David is he's such a gamer. He'll try anything for the cause. I remember wanting him to spice up and humanize *Taking the Pledge,* a special we were doing for the Discovery Channel. In no time at all, he and Tara improvised a backstage scene with David griping about having to do too much housework and Tara griping that he was never around long enough to do any at all. Hilarious! This, from a couple of superidealis-tic PhDs. No wonder David was recently voted one of the greatest Canadians in history. A scientist? How improbable is that? And when I call to congratulate him, he shrugs it off, saying (with his tongue in his cheek) he's much more excited by the poll of women who voted him the man they most wanted to be marooned on a desert island with. Well, what do you expect from a geneticist who appears on the cover of *TV Guide* wearing nothing but a fig leaf (albeit a large one)?

But if you really want to know David, go camping with him. Up north, in the wild country. Hang with the Haida Nation, the original British Columbians—they're all his friends. Take a hike in the rain forest, sit around the camp-fire, listen to his stories, tell him yours. And, for heaven's sake, go fishing with him. That's the only thing, other than the environment, that he takes really seriously.

We're lucky to have David Suzuki, aren't we? I mean living here on Planet Earth with us. He could have chosen any other planet, but he chose ours. So maybe we'll be around for a bit longer. If we listen to David...

THE WRAP

*N*ow, where are we? oh, yes— the ending for my nonmemoir. It's a happy one, of course, with a beloved wife and a super bunch of kids, living in a land without winter and enjoying my chosen profession for half a century. "Happy is the man who's found his work and one good woman to love." Amen.

But suppose I told you—in the strictest of confidence— that I had an ulterior motive. That I didn't just want to create dreams for people, make them laugh, distract them from the cruel exigencies of life. Not that that isn't enough. It is, and it's what makes my profession an honorable one. But it was never enough for me. So my secret is this: I've always wanted to influence people. Some of my shows have been seen by half a billion people. How did it affect them? Did the young people who watched the show with Danny Kaye at the Metropolitan Opera find opera a little more accessible, a little less daunting? Hope so. Was Helen Hunt's Kathy Miller the model of courage we can all emulate? Hope so. Was Nureyev's performance in *Invitation to the Dance* just another star turn, or did folks get it when Julie sang "Anyone can do it / Anyone can dance"? Hope so. Did they get it when Suzuki told them on *Global Dreams* the DNA from prehistoric animals isn't much different from yours and mine? That all us animals are in it together? Hope so. I've spent many a night tossing and turning, wondering if some scene I shot that day might be misinterpreted and have a negative impact on viewers. Either way, you never know. Except once.

I was very proud of the film I produced about a family with an autistic child and how they cured him. The film won us many awards, but the medical profession was up in arms. They said autism couldn't be cured.

Some years later, my friend Sandra sent me a magazine article about another little boy whose family had cured him of autism. The little boy, now normal, was interviewed and asked what had turned him around. His reply was that a film he had watched on television with his family inspired them, gave them hope.

So there it was. Something I produced really helped someone.

Were there others? Hope so.

INDEX